Seeing Past Z

ALSO BY BETH KEPHART

A Slant of Sun: One Child's Courage
Into the Tangle of Friendship
Still Love in Strange Places

Seeing Past Z

Nurturing the Imagination in a Fast-Forward World

Beth Kephart

W. W. Norton & Company

NEW YORK / LONDON

For information about permission to reproduce selections from this book, write to
Permissions, W. W. Norton & Company, Inc., 500 Fifth Avenue, New York, NY 10110

Manufacturing by Courier Westford
Book design by Brooke Koven
Production manager: Anna Oler

Library of Congress Cataloging-in-Publication Data
Kephart, Beth.
Seeing past Z : nurturing the imagination in a fast-forward world /
Beth Kephart.— 1st ed.
p. cm.
ISBN 0-393-05882-4 (hardcover)
1. Creative thinking—Anecdotes. 2. Imagination—Anecdotes. 3. Kephart, Beth.
I. Title.
LB1062.K43 2004
370.15'7—dc22

2004001106

W. W. Norton & Company, Inc., 500 Fifth Avenue, New York, N.Y. 10110
www.wwnorton.com

W. W. Norton & Company Ltd., Castle House, 75/76 Wells Street, London W1T 3QT

1 2 3 4 5 6 7 8 9 0

For Jeremy,
who sees way past Z.

And for my parents,
who gave me room to dream and love to grow on.

Imagination has given us the steam engine, the telephone, the talking machine, and the automobile, for these things had to be dreamed of before they became realities. So I believe that dreams—daydreams, you know, with your eyes wide open and your brain machinery whizzing—are likely to lead to the betterment of the world. The imaginative child will become the imaginative man or woman most apt to invent, and therefore to foster, civilization.

—L. FRANK BAUM

Think left and think right and think low and think high.
Oh the thinks you can think up if only you try!

—THEODORE GEISEL

Contents

Acknowledgments

A debt of gratitude is owed to the magazine and newspaper editors who have given me space in their respective pages, a place to lodge some of the early thoughts that coalesced, over time, into *Seeing Past Z*. Among them: Marie Arana, Miriam Arond, John Darnton, Don George, Stephen Fried, Gary Kamiya, Nora Krug, Adam Langer, Laura Miller, John Prendergast, Elizabeth Taylor, and Amy Virshup.

A debt is owed as well to those whose intelligience, grace, and friendship have been indispensable throughout the shaping of these pages—Robb Forman Dew, Ivy Goodman, Alyson Hagy, Katrina Kenison, Kate Moses, Jayne Anne Phillips, Karen Rile, Rahna Reiko Rizzuto, and Susan Straight—and to Dave Mendell, Lisa Roper, and Lisa's son, Jake Summers, who shared a story and a poem with gracious enthusiasm.

I will always be grateful to the kids who read and wrote and thought out loud with me during so many workshop nights. You are, all of you, dear to me and entirely unforgettable.

Thank you as always to Amy Rennert, who has helped guide my dreams to print ever since I stepped into the land of literature with my own unbridled imagination, who makes me laugh when I need to laugh, and who brings a clear eye and a steady hand to the blessed and baffling business of books.

A thank you as well to Alane Salierno Mason, who saw a glimmer of a story in the early pages, held fast to her vision of what this book might be, and sent a gorgeous bouquet one April afternoon. Gratitude for Alessandra Bastagli for her unerring sensibility and timing. Many thanks to Mary Babcock for a wise red pencil, and to Kimberly Glyder for just the right cover.

Finally, to the men in my life, Bill and Jeremy: For inspiring, for enduring, for listening, and for loving, for the startling gift of an orange jasmine tree.

Seeing Past Z

Imagining Tomorrow

*T*HIS IS WHAT he looks like: dark lustrous hair and big curious eyes, cinnamon or chocolate eyes, eyes like phosphorescence. A young runner's body and fidgeting hands, a south-side dent in either eyebrow, a brilliant white scar inside the thatch of his hair, and a smile that's not big enough for the way you sense he's feeling. Tell him a joke, and he'll laugh out loud. Help him strap on a pair of Rollerblades, and he'll gather speed and fly.

The night he was conceived, it rained. The next morning I knew, intuitively knew, that I was carrying a boy. No ultrasound would deliver the news. No doctor would confirm it. But I saw a boy's black curls and chubby hands. I saw pillow cheeks and dirty knees—a son, I saw a son.

What I didn't see and couldn't predict was how radically this son would change me, how my politics and dreams and language would soon be filtered through my fierce love for him. Nor did I anticipate how much time I'd spend reflecting on what a parent *is* and what parents *do*, which battles must be joined and won, which positions articulated and defended. Jeremy was conceived on a blue-tinged night. It's been all weather ever since—magnificent and pounding.

Nine years into motherhood, I understand that I am living on the margins—of child-rearing books, of culture. In a world in which children of a certain privileged class are made to jockey for acceptance to "elite" nursery schools, ten-year-old kids are having anxiety breakdowns, and preparation for college admission begins before puberty, I have been seeking, above all else, a conversation with my son. In an era in which the competition for "gifted" academic programs yields a new color of prejudice, I have been placing my faith in words and the silences between them, looking for story in the rhythms of our lives, believing in the power of literature to inform, instruct, shape, and broaden; to shield, preserve, enlighten. I have been pursuing ordinary happiness when *ordinary* is not purported to suffice, when the soul itself doesn't seem to count for much, when the magazines and some teachers and those proverbial parents down the street seem entirely hell-bent on quantifying the child—sharpening skills at the expense of reverie, building dossiers instead of memories, compromising childhood with adult concerns and competitions. Woe to the kid who plays the tuba or colors the sky red. Woe to the kid with the free afternoon in a community obsessed with lessons.

Jeremy is black haired, great eyed, trusting; a collector of details; a mimic of voices; a fan of the bedtime inquiry and small confession. He likes to talk at a slow, emphatic pace, and he likes to solve the problems that he cranks up for himself, spectacularly original puzzles. Through toddlerhood and childhood, I have watched my son reach out, laugh loud, and locate—it was not easy at first—language, confidence, friends. I have gone upstairs to find him engulfed by Lilliputian cities (plastic drawbridges, castles, cannons, three-inch-high knights, and proportionate armor) or by roadways crammed with miniature cars, and I have watched him establish his own precipitous plans, learn the joy of decoding a fantastic pun. There's hardly a detail Jeremy doesn't remember—dates, colors, names, the nuances of long-ago conversations are rarely lost on him—and my kid was born with such an instinct for politeness, such a certain equation for decency and kindness that I am often caught off guard, shamed by my own impatience and quick judgments. He loves projects, always has. He loves putting things in the order he deems just right and entertaining the thoughts in his head and exercising his right to an infinity of moods. *He is Kind. Understanding. Funny. Honest. Fair. Has good ideas. Has different moods*, a little strawberry blonde wrote of him recently, and I think she has it just about right; that's who he is, at the moment. My job as his parent is the job of every parent—to keep giving him more of the world. To thread it in and through, strand by annealing, instructive strand. To make room for him to marvel, shift, consider, and weigh; to enter other people's stories and begin to tell his own.

I want to raise my son to pursue wisdom over winning. I want him to channel his passions and talents and personal politics into rivers of his choosing. I'd like to take the chance that I feel it is my right to take on contentment over credentials, imagination over conquest, the idiosyncratic point of view over the standard-issue one. I'd like to live in a world where that's okay.

Some call this folly. Some make a point of reminding me of all the most relevant data: That the imagination has lost its standing in classrooms and families nationwide. That storytelling is for those with too much time. That winning early is one bet-hedging path toward winning later on. That there isn't time, as there once was time, for a child's inner life. That a mother who eschews competition for conversation is a mother who places her son at risk for second-class citizenry.

Perhaps. But I have this boy with these two huge dark eyes who thinks and plays and speculates. I have a boy who is emergent and hopeful, intuitive and funny, somewhere between childhood and adolescence. How will he define himself as the years unfold? What will he claim as his own? What will he craft out of the past? What will he do with what he thinks, make of what he dreams, invent out of the stuff of all his passions? It is my right—it is my obligation, even—to sit with him for a while longer, imagining tomorrow.

I'll Trade You My Story
for Your Story

WE ARE SIDE by side, on a crowded, midmorning train. I am the orphaned wizard, Harry Potter, and also Potter's cousin, Dudley, and also Dumbledore and Hagrid. Jeremy, for his part, is my nine-year-old kid—looking out the window, watching the trees blur by, thinking his thoughts, tuning in and out of the tale.

"*Harry picked [the letter] up and stared at it, his heart twanging like a giant elastic band,*" I read. "*No one, ever, in his whole life, had written to him. Who would?*" The train slows and speeds, loses some passengers, gains new ones. I read about Harry and his hard luck, Harry and his change of luck, the extraordinary circumstances of Harry's magic life. I read loud enough that two kids, four rows up, leave their mother to stand at my side, so that now there are four of us in Harry's world, together, heading east.

"Mom," Jeremy interrupts.

"Yes?" My normal voice.

"Harry's aunt and uncle are lousy. And Hagrid: He might be a little weird."

"Well, I can stop reading," I tell him, "if you want me to."

"No," Jeremy says. "Actually. I want to know what happens. Don't stop." Settling differently against my arm, now watching not the window, but the book. He follows every word I read, and so I read like Broadway. I read through six or seven stops and then through the eighth, where the brother and sister who stand in the aisle heed their mother's instructions and detrain. When I look up, I encounter the two full moons of Jeremy's eyes. "I can see it," he says. "I really can."

"What do you see?"

"Harry. In my mind. Just like a movie."

I read some more, then close the book, kiss the white scar beneath the thatch of Jeremy's hair. The train groans and I do not speak, for this is certainly enough for now, this is Jeremy lodged inside another's tale, and now that he has been transported, I leave him to it. The train slogs on, jangles and yawns. We see the backs of houses, the start of leaves, the abandonment of old Christmas trees thrown up against the train tracks. We see other lives and other stories staring back at us.

I want to know what happens. Don't stop. I play Jeremy's words over in my head, think of how long I've waited to hear them, of how many stories I've read aloud on trains and couches and the back lawn, of how I've urged and pleaded. *Listen to this story, let me tell you this story, I'll trade you my story for your story.*

But Jeremy liked his own thoughts better. He liked the theater of make-believe figures that he moved around the floor. He liked to collect facts and solve puzzles and manipulate projects, and if I have given him room for all that and more, if I have respected the privacy of his fantasies and thoughts, I have also persisted with these stories. I have asked him to trust me, to believe that other people's stories matter, to join me in the unfamiliar, the unknown. "Why?" he has wanted to know, an honest question. Asking it while he played with his plastic men or compiled his statistics or streaked ahead of me on rainbow-colored Rollerblades. Because stories enlarge our sense of the possible, I've said. They give us new questions to answer. They enable us to better see the gnarly stuff beneath the surface, let us see what the future might hold, if we keep ourselves wise and open to it. Stories feed our imagination, I say, and imagination takes us, in the words of Dr. Seuss, beyond the letter Z. "Just let me read to you, okay?" I've said, and Jeremy's shrugged. "Okay," but nothing's moved him.

I failed with *Charlotte's Web*. I got nowhere with *The Chronicles of Narnia*. I couldn't get a nip of interest with *The Borrowers*. I was starting to wonder if there is indeed a story for every child, if I was going to fail at this, if I'd have to find another way—there are always other ways—to reflect out loud with Jeremy, to broaden and color his perspective. But then I carried *Harry Potter and the Sorcerer's Stone* onto a train. I started reading out loud about a quirky kid with a blazing white scar and potent, untapped powers, and I watched a velvet curtain being pulled across a stage. *I want to know what happens. Don't stop.* And here Jeremy sits considering the enticements, the perils, the nascent friendships, the mysterious past of a character named Harry.

Tomorrow, I think, we will read again. We will move forward with Harry—look for the implied stomp of the foot, the huff, the conspiracy, the dance, the cringe, the charming repetition. We will incline our ears toward discovery, dare. We will lift the letters from the page and yield to the images we conjure up and size up the risks and consequences. We will wander off this story's path and look at surfaces and depths, lost souls and triumph, the mechanics and mist of forgiveness, the immutability of the past, the love that lives after parents pass on, and in all this reading of someone else's story, we'll look for parts of us. But for now all that matters is that a train is jangling east. That a world is coming into focus, and now it blurs, and now again it sharpens and blurs.

Tiny Golden Spark

"YOU MIGHT THINK," I read, "*if you didn't know him well, that he was a stern and serious man. He wasn't. He was actually a wildly funny person. What made him appear so serious was the fact that he never smiled with his mouth. He did it all with his eyes. He had brilliant blue eyes and when he thought of something funny, his eyes would flash and, if you looked carefully, you could actually see a tiny golden spark dancing in the middle of each eye. But the mouth never moved.*"

"Wait," Jeremy says.

"What?"

"Read it again."

It's a midspring blue-sky day. On opposing deck chairs, Jeremy and I sit, his feet on my lap, my own feet slung off to one side. If Jeremy came to *Danny the Champion of the World* with reinforcements—a grape Popsicle, a bottle of water—he has been peaceably inside this effusive, chummy Roald Dahl tale since I turned the first page, thoroughly taken with Danny and his father, just as he allowed himself, only a few weeks ago, to be thoroughly taken with a kid named Harry. This is a frame I long to freeze. Jeremy likes the fact that the characters live in a "real old gypsy wagon," likes what he can imagine of the father's filling station, likes the way Danny's father loves Danny enough to compensate for the fact of the missing mother. Jeremy likes that these characters are flawed (they have vices!) but kind, that they live without much but don't seem to complain—even about the rustic toilet. When I repeat the part about the smiling eyes, Jeremy raises his Popsicle like an index finger.

"Mom?"

"Yes?"

"This is interesting."

"Why?"

"Because Danny and his father remind me of me and Dad."

"They do?" I ask, because my husband is an architect, not the owner of a filling station, and because there are two real toilets in our non-gypsy-wagon house, and because my husband doesn't have a private vice, at least one that I'm aware of, and because, after all, there is a mother here; I didn't die when my boy was four months old.

"They do."

"Why's that?"

"Because Danny and his father like to be together, and that's the same with me and Dad. And besides, it's interesting about the way the father smiles."

"How so?"

"Because I don't know if I can smile like that, but I'm pretty sure that Dad can. I think he does sometimes smile like that. Not with his mouth, but with his eyes."

"Hmm," I say, and try to think of my husband smiling. His freckled part-Salvadoran, part-Filipino, part-Italian, part-Spanish, part-American face. His eyes (so brown, not even close to blue) and the way they sit, on his prominent, enviable cheekbones. Golden spark. Yes, I've seen it flare between them. When he tells Jeremy a joke only the two of them can understand. When they share the same secret they're determined to keep from me. "Do you want to see if you can do it?" I ask, though the question is unnecessary, for Jeremy is way ahead of me here—not just looking past the particulars to the heart of the story, but making diverting faces in the sun. He chews his lips to keep them from breaking into a smile. He widens and narrows his eyes in pursuit of the tiny golden spark.

"Am I smiling yet?" he asks me, through pursed lips, but he looks so funny that I can't help laughing, and now he is laughing too.

"Now you are," I say. "Now you're smiling."

"No." He laughs. "Before. With my eyes."

"Well," I say, "Danny says that you can't fake it. Listen." And then I read the very next sentences in the book, the ones that further instruct about smiles: *"I was glad my father was an eye-smiler. It meant he never gave me a fake smile because it's impossible to make your eyes twinkle if you aren't feeling twinkly yourself. A mouth-smile is different. You can fake a mouth-smile any time you want, simply by moving your lips. I've also learned that a real mouth-smile always has an eye-smile to go with it. So watch out, I say, when someone smiles at you with his mouth but his eyes stay the same. It's sure to be a phony."*

"Well," Jeremy says. He's looking past me, to the yard. "Do you know what I think?"

"What?"

"That people look best when they smile. You, for example, look much much prettier when you smile."

"Is that right?" I say, genuinely taken aback, not sure which is the more profound revelation—that my son has thought, in the privacy of his own head, about the way I look when I smile, or that he has considered what happens to my face in the absence of joy or satisfaction.

"It's much better when you smile." Jeremy is emphatic. "Much." He looks at me as if he's never noticed a line in my face, never looked for evidence of age or considered the possibility. All he seems to see, at the moment, is mood and soul, happiness or its opposite, and all I see is how preposterously blessed I am to be having this conversation about smiling in the sun, this glimpse of myself through my only child's eyes. We haven't gotten to the moral dilemmas yet, to the questions of right or wrong, to Dahl's final message to the reader: "When you grow up and have children of your own, do please remember something important. A stodgy parent is no fun at all!" But still here we are, deep in, *committed* to Danny and his father, who might cheat a little, who might steal and get in trouble, but whose hearts are good and who measure honesty by the way they love each other.

That night when Bill comes home and asks Jeremy for an update on the day, he gets the usual about homework, recess, cafeteria lines. He gets Jeremy's genuine questions back, and then he gets Jeremy with something more he wants to say. Pausing theatrically the way that he does, shaping the air with his hands, Jeremy begins to tell his dad about Roald Dahl's Danny. Bill hears the stuff about the gypsy caravan and no toilets. He hears about the BFG and smiling eyes. He hears, as I hear, Jeremy's neural networks churning—all the clinkings and sputterings and word searches in between, for he is young and new to storytelling.

I watch it happen. I listen as Jeremy converts and translates, leaves some things out, overemphasizes others, starts laughing before he gets to the punch lines. Dahl's story has all of a sudden taken a reverberatory turn—as Jeremy tells it, he shifts it, and as Bill listens, it shifts again, until there are three stories in this room: the one Dahl wrote, the one Jeremy tells, and the one Bill conjures up for himself. And then there's this story of the sharing of stories, which would be a different story altogether were it retold by my husband or my son.

But I'm doing the recording for now. I am sitting across from these two, taking note. I am thinking that a story is great if we feel impelled to pass it on, but a story is even finer when a child slips between its lines and takes possession of it. Acts it out, interprets it, retells it, injects it with a few harmless lies of his own. We lie our way right up to the truth in the act of sharing stories. We exaggerate, we understate, we choose a side, defend it.

Legacies

C LOSE TO THE end of third grade, Jeremy comes home
with an announcement. He will be performing in the
class play, *Stone Soup*, delivering a specified cache of
lines. He's not a guy who goes in for costumes, he says, and he's
not planning on much of a disguise.

He goes upstairs; I hear him reciting. I stay downstairs, busy
with work. When I call up to him after some time has passed, he
calls back that he is fine, he's got his lines stashed in memory.
"When's the show?" I ask him now.

"Next week," he answers. No nerves.

All week long it is just like that—no nerves. We walk home
from his school in the afternoon, and he tells funny stories, he's
relaxed. He does his homework fast, then skips out to play, his
shoes untied, his shirttail flapping. A friend from another neighborhood stops by, and they do the things they tend to do when this
boy has time to visit—lip-sync in the family room, trade a Jolly

Rancher for two Starbursts, pound a ball in the backyard. I stand at the sink or sit in my office or pull the weeds out of the lawn, and every now and then I hear the stuff of their talk—talk about kids and school, the coming summer, hiding places. It's when I'm walking from my office to the kitchen that I realize that they're upstairs now, and cackling. I pause at the bottom of the steps to listen to the noise in the room above my head.

It takes me a moment to figure out that Jeremy is reading to his friend—performing a page from *Wayside School Is Falling Down*. He is reading the words the way the author, Louis Sachar, has written the words, *acting* them, with the hyphenations, the all-cap beats, the extravagant exasperations. It's a scene in which a new student has been misidentified by his teacher, and the boy has to summon his courage to tell the teacher the truth. The only problem is that the boy himself has trouble with his name. Both the *Benjamin* and the *Nushmutt* are problematic. He knows what's going down. He's been humiliated in the past. Strangers simply refuse to understand him.

"And what's your name, little boy?" an adult would ask him.
"Benjamin Nushmutt," he'd answer.
"What?"
"BENjamin NUSHmutt."
"What?"
"Ben-Ja-Min Nush-Mutt."
"What?"
"BenjaMIN NushMUTT!"
"What?"
"Benjamin Nushmutt."
"Oh, nice to meet you, Benjamin."
He never knew what it was that made the person suddenly understand.

Upstairs Jeremy is trying hard to read this passage without laughing. He gets to "Nush," and he cracks up. He gets to

"MUTT," and he is gone. "Let me see," Jeremy's friend keeps saying, and then the friend tries to read the page, but he gets jumbled up with laughter, and then I can't tell which one is which, who is sucking air and who is coughing it, who is smothering his laughter in the carpet. I wish I could go up there and stand in the doorway and watch these kids—the one of them dark haired, the other one blond, the one a former reluctant reader, the other an athlete with a notorious pitching arm—go to pieces over Sachar, but it doesn't matter what I see. It matters that it's happening, that a book is filling this moment with something eminently silly. If the *Oxford Shorter* says innocence is freedom from sin or guilt, I say innocence is this.

A few days later, Jeremy's pleasure in the Wayside School series increases manifold when the mail arrives and there's a letter for him from the author himself—a response to some fan mail Jeremy had penned a few weeks before. "Thanks for your very nice letter," Sachar's note begins. "I'm glad you like my books so much. *Sideways Stories from Wayside School* was my first book. I wrote it in 1976. I didn't know if it would be published or if anyone would ever read it. I used to look like Louis, the yard teacher. Now I look more like that mysterious bald man who keeps showing up. . . ."

"He used to look like Louis." Jeremy stops right there, looks up from the typed page. "Like Louis!"

"What do you know?" I say.

"But now he looks more like the bald man."

"Maybe he's just being modest."

"So, he's like two of the characters in his own fiction books," Jeremy continues. "Two of them, at the same time." He runs upstairs to get the books. He comes back down to show me the yard teacher and the bald man and to try to figure out how one writer could be two characters at once. It's a question that Jeremy would never be considering if the author had not taken the time to write this note, to reach out to a young reader with a story about the story.

There are so many books in the world to be celebrated and shared, and then there are the souls who lead us to them. In this case we have Jeremy's librarian to thank—the gentle and great Mr. Stever, who doesn't just dress the parts of the characters in the stories he performs—look for him and you'll find a prince, you'll find a joker, you'll find a dragon or Robin Hood—but who makes it a point to so genuinely befriend his students that he has something in perpetual store for each of them. A stack of books for the boy who likes spiders and a recommendation for the girl who likes the fantastic and a suggestion for the dark-haired, vaguely Latin kid, my son, who says a good book makes you laugh. Mr. Stever's library is purple and green, alive with effulgent things that dangle from the ceiling and stuffed creatures that sit plopped against the shelves. In his office are the crown, the cape, the hats, the slippers that transform him into fiction. On his shelves are the books fourth-graders write, books he prizes like the newest Caldecotts. His library changes mood as the sun presses in, and beside the pillows there are open spaces in which the kids can sprawl and often do, a book beneath their chins. Take the story home, Mr. Stever says. Read it. Share it. Tell me how you liked it later.

As much as Mr. Stever knows, as smart as he most assuredly is, it's his enthusiasm for the *idea* of story that makes him rare, his genius at matching rhyme or plot with child. Mr. Stever's legacy is the legacy of gifts—the legacy of awe or wonder or humor passed on, from a man to a child to a friend. There is always, for this librarian, the room for story. There is always the need for it, the opportunity. In Mr. Stever's world, stories—the ones in books as well as the ones that are made up on the spot—perform countless acts of magic and even sometimes heal, and he is never too preoccupied to miss a chance to encourage the kids to imagine stories of their own.

Dear Jeremy, Mr. Stever wrote one day after Jeremy had left a handmade puppet in the library office for Mr. Stever's son who had not, Jeremy knew, been well. *One day I opened the envelope and your puppet was inside. I knew it was a puppet you had made and I knew it took a long time and that you worked very hard to put it together. It made a big smile come to my face. I began to make silly voices to make it talk. I knew right away that David would be the first person I would show it to. That night I took it to the hospital, and David and his mom and I all laughed at some of the funny rhymes and stories we made up. When I was driving home that night I knew I wanted to find something to let you know how special I think you are. When I found the green soccer bear I thought about you right away. I know how much you love soccer, and the color fits perfectly with your hat story. I hope you will have fun and maybe some good adventures and stories will come to your mind as you play with him.*

WHEN THE DAY of the *Stone Soup* performance comes to pass, I realize that Mrs. Hendrix, Jeremy's third-grade teacher, has infected her class with that same emphatic, democratic dream of passing a story on, that Jeremy has not shown any signs of nerves, preperformance, because there has simply been no need. If this dear-hearted, broad-minded teacher has encouraged the kids to find the lessons in the folktale, worked on vocabulary, instructed about spelling, she has also made it clear to them that they are, one and all, essential—that every one of them is necessary to relay the story of stones and soup to the parents who will gather. *Stone Soup* is an equal-opportunity play—the few spoken lines by peasants and soldiers are well distributed, every character in the famine-stricken country is hungry, the ploy of adding stones to a pot of boiling water and then asking for mere "garnishes" has a familiar *Emperor's New Clothes* quality to it. For it to work as a production, the kids must enter the story, appeal to one another, prompt, make way, support, remind with a raised eyebrow or an elbow. They must trust, when they climb up on the stage, that together they make narrative.

And that's what happens when the kids-cum-soldiers-and-peasants trundle through the cafeteria side door and up to the elementary-school stage at the designated hour. They stand before the assembled mothers, fathers, grandmothers, and baby-sitters, and plastic helmets bang, and laden backpacks slouch, and kerchiefs slip from the heads of girls. Everyone who needs one has a shiny polished stone or a head of cabbage or a bunch of carrots or some zingy, springy parsley, and by the time they've taken their practiced places on that stage, there's no going back, no brushing up, no stopping one of the actors from tossing his script faceup into the cauldron and leaning down to read from a bent knee.

But best of all, from my perspective, is that there is no headliner on this cafeteria stage. No anointed prima donna, no extras standing on the sidelines, no one who has won momentary fame at the expense of any other. Isn't this the way it ought to be at this age? No nerves, no competition, no bruised egos, no inflated self-importance, nothing but community and self-esteem, nothing but kids in possession of a story. What has been learned here is a story about hunger and the power of suggestion. What has been taught is that a class can make a play, that narrative forges society, that there is still room for every child upon an attenuating stage.

Guess Who

"HEY, MOM," JEREMY says one late June morning, in school-less summer. "Do you want to play Guess Who?"

"Guess Who?" I say. "But didn't we play that yesterday?"

"So?"

"And the day before that and also on Monday?"

"It's a great game, Mom. What does it matter?"

"It's just . . ." I start, then stop. "It's just that I'm bored with Guess Who?"

"That's impossible," Jeremy says emphatically. "You can't get bored with Guess Who? Look," he says, dragging the game box out of the pantry and plunking it down on the kitchen table. "What could be boring about this?"

He removes the lid of the Milton Bradley box to reveal the twenty-four mystery faces on the twenty-four yellow cards, the two game boards, and the two scorekeepers. The object of the game, to directly quote the instructions, is "to guess the Mystery Person on your opponent's card by asking one question per turn, and eliminating any game-board faces that don't fit the Mystery Person's description." This means, in other words, that you spend the morning asking questions like: Does your Mystery Person have a beard? Does your Mystery Person wear a hat? Is your Mystery Person a bottle blonde? Is he or she vision impaired?

It's a process-of-elimination game, and Jeremy, who takes a detective's pleasure in asking the most strategic questions at the most opportune junctures, wins hands down every time. He loves zeroing in on the case. He loves exclaiming "aha!" after acquiring each new clue.

"You really don't want to play?" he asks, after delivering his best sales pitch and looking up into my silence.

"Tomorrow?" I say. "Or the next day?" Feeling the rush of guilt I always feel in long summer stretches or winter breaks about having a single child on a now-childless street, no cousins nearby for him to play with. When I walk away from one of his invitations, I feel the weight of the word *stranded*. Still, as my mother used to say, the greatest gift in life is the capacity to entertain oneself. It's a talent that cannot evolve without ample time and practice.

"Okay, Mom," Jeremy says, and he starts digging into the box— pulling out all the yellow cards and arranging the faces into piles. Soon the entire kitchen table is a mosaic of Guess Who? I wonder if he's understood that I haven't been persuaded. I don't intend to play.

"Tomorrow?" I repeat.

"Sure," he mumbles.

"So what are you doing?" I ask.

"Playing." Jeremy doesn't look up and is not inclined to offer more details. I watch his slender fingers work the cards. He puts balding Sam beside behatted Bernard. He pairs rhinestone Claire with the evil-seeming Philip. Pointy-chin Eric is slotted beside square-glasses Joe. Alfred, looking like a nineteenth-century castoff, is out there on his own.

"Sounds good," I say.

"Yup," Jeremy says. And I leave him to his game.

A FEW HOURS LATER, the Guess Who? cards and the kitchen table are obscured by scraps of scribbled-upon paper. Blobs of wet ink decorate Jeremy's hands. He looks exhausted, frankly, his dark hair pushed up into ridges on his head, and he doesn't see me until I'm standing right there beside him, touching my finger to his cheek.

"What's going on?" I ask quietly.

"Guess Who?" he says.

My silence is the question.

"Well, the game makers only gave the characters first names," Jeremy starts, exhaling deeply after a pregnant pause. "But I think they need last names, too. So I did that. And I also think that they need jobs," he goes on, "so now they have them. And I'm working on addresses and phone numbers. I'm going to make a phone book."

Jeremy lifts up each corresponding scrap of paper as he speaks, brandishing the pages for my benefit. The last names: Sam *Douglas*, Bernard *Scholl*, Charles *Frocks*, Max *Plape*, Herman *Scholl*, Paul *Mankle*, George *Tobleck*, David *Neftrick*. The jobs: anything from factory owner, hunter, or restaurateur to the moneytaker at the tollbooth plaza. The phone numbers: all effectively area-code correct, reflecting the characters' wide-ranging domiciles.

"Bernard and Herman both have the same last name," I observe lamely, while I try to think of something smart to say.

"They're German," Jeremy says. "And they're cousins."

"Do they have wives?" I ask.

"I'm going to decide on that tomorrow."

Silence again. Jeremy leans his head against the chair.

"And after that, I'm going to put them on *Saturday Night Live*."

"You are."

"Yeah. They are going to compete. You know, with jokes. David Neftrick's going to tell an inventing joke and Max Plape is going to tell a meat-and-vegetables joke. Charles Frocks is going to win. His joke is going to be about painting."

"Well that's a show I'd like to see," I say.

"You can if you want to," Jeremy says. "I'll tell you curtain time."

Jeremy sighs again and pushes out his chair. "I'm going upstairs to hang out," he tells me. "I'm pretty tired." He scratches his face, smudging a dull black bruise of ink above one eye. He leaves everything on the table, strewn right where it is—the mosaic of cards and the game boards and the scraps of paper and the pens. "Don't touch it," he says to me. "Okay? It took me too long to get this far."

He lets me brush his ink-bruised forehead with a kiss before he stands, cuts a diagonal across the kitchen, and takes the steps two at a time. Now it's me who is alone at the kitchen table, with these characters that have been conjured into life. The last names kind of fit, I think. And the German cousins do look German. And if anybody is going to tell a meat-and-vegetables joke, it'll be Max. That's just the way it is and the way it's going to be. I leave the mosaic on the table as the inventor has directed.

Dimming the Lights

W E DRIVE FOR many days over the thin carapace of the earth, beneath a vast and vaporous sky. It is August, the end of the sunflower season. Like tired corn, the stalks take their beating from the sun—their faces the color of repentance, their fringes singed past glory. Where there are no flowers, there are loose-jowled cows, and where the cows have given ground, there are flocks of indifferent sheep, and sometimes as we drive there is no ground at all. It's rocks on one side, and nothing but air on the other. "Bill," I say to the man at the wheel. "For God's sake, Bill, we're going to fall." And then, because God has intervened, we are miraculously spared.

Earth, in this southwest knuckle of France, is a phantasma of layers. It is our planet left essentially alone, or perhaps more truthfully, it is our planet respected. Ruined stone castles crumble down hills. Iron crosses sprout out of unlikely limestone pilings. I come from a place where land has been disregarded, pulped, and here, in this region of unblemished possibility, I suffer from a sadness that is also partly prayer.

Can you read the world as you read a book? Can you see in stalks and cows and sheep and rock a telling narrative? Can you teach a child? Can a child teach you? In southern France, we have been thinking of Thoreau: "It's not what you look at that matters, it's what you see." We have been hunting for details, patterns, and surprises, making lists and trading them, reflecting on our capacity to bear witness: Not just to the moon but to the haunting power of the moon. Not just to the dying of the sunflowers but to the fact of so many embedded seeds. Not just to the thick, stone, age-old houses but to the way those houses come alive.

I want Jeremy to grow up poking his fingers through the web of mysteries, hoping for the unexpected, taking pleasure or conviction or understanding from what he finds. I want him to build the bridges we all must learn to build between the world we are taught and the world we read about and the world we will only ever guess at. Curiosity bolsters knowledge, and knowledge feeds intelligence, and intelligence helps us navigate our lives—that is the way it works—and so we are here looking for the cloud of flour above the baker's shop. For the miniature dogs in the baskets of bikes. For the color of river water to change depending on the light. For the cows to crowd into shady wedges, for boys to head off with fishing poles, for the rain to come at night. We have gone from town to town in southern France, teaching ourselves to pay attention, to see—the domestic and the sacred, the glorified and the wasted, the crumble of a castle and the wedding in the street. Reading the world as if it were a book so that tomorrow or the next day the stories we imagine, tell, act out, or write will pay homage right back to the world.

On the day we leave for La Grotte Rose, the valleys are obscured by fog. It burns off before noon, and by then we are already too far gone along a narrow necklace of road to turn back.

Closing my eyes, I leave the navigation to Bill and the entertainment to Jeremy, who is doing a fair impersonation of Ricky Martin in the back of the rented Renault. At one hairpin curve some 860 meters up, Bill swerves and curses a camper barreling down wide on the single-lane road. I put one hand over my eyes and sip the air. When the earth decides to level out again, I open my eyes to find a gunmetal landscape, and evergreens that are stumpy and ill shapen. We pass through a town big enough to have a name and small enough to be contained in a single photo. The roofs of its five houses scrape against the ground, while a battalion of white geese honk their opinion.

The caves, when we reach them, are ancient and startling, too. We are offered former visitors' discarded sweaters to wear, for it is cold—ten degrees—inside the earth. We are given the history, which sounds like folklore, about a shepherd named Sahuquet who, one crisp day in the autumn of 1880, saw a fox enter a fissure in the rocks. Being the good shepherd he must have been, Sahuquet set off in pursuit, fitting himself between the stones. It wasn't until his eyes adjusted to the light that he saw the ghosts knocking their heads against the smooth domed ceiling, the colored magic wands thrusting up from the netherlands. When he screamed, the ghosts screamed back, and this, of course, was Hell. Vowing never to return, Sahuquet never did. But he told his friends what he had seen and heard, and soon others brought the craft of speleology to the caves.

In the sun, we fiddle with our adopted sweaters until the tour guide, his story over, finally steps aside to let us through. Inside the caves, the air seems more wet than cool, and we pull our arms in toward our chests, like birds settling their wings. There must be two dozen of us on this tour, and when I turn around there is already no sign of sun behind us, no evidence of the gray-green tundra, or of the nasty gap at the edge of the cliff. Claustrophobia has no business here. Over the next damp hour, we will walk inside the belly of the earth. I will ask Jeremy to look, to really see.

We go 120 meters down. And down. We see galactic creatures, depths. It is as if we are looking at a church, and then a tortoise, and then a minaret, these shapes molded out of stalactites and stalagmites. Some structures are like needles, and some are like small-capped mushrooms, and some are like the free-form sand castles I used to pour through my fingers beside the tide pools at the shore. The guide speaks to us in French, a language we hardly know, and so Bill and I explain the creatures to ourselves, then do our best translations for Jeremy. Rainwater is not neutral, but acid, we say. It creeps between rock layers, it trickles and gropes—breaking the earth's surface into clints and grikes and sinkholes, opening tunnels into which streams may disappear. It runs underground, and it dissolves rocks, and it chisels out networks, passages, tunnels, caves, caverns, domes, like these domes. Rainwater alone, dissolving the calcite of limestone, yields a single color, white, we say. But where there is ferrous oxide, there are red, yellow, and pink. Where there is manganese oxide, there are charcoal and gray. There is an explanation for all of this. An explanation. Sort of.

Down we go, farther down. "Eeww la la," Jeremy whispers. "Eeww la la," in his very best French, with the awe of childhood. I fumble around with my camera, knowing no photo can succeed. The colors will be wrong, and how do you photograph *glisten*, anyway? How do you train your lens to measure the distance between yourself and a sky of stone? We go farther down, past a church pulpit, a flock of sheep, a forest of candles, something the guide calls the chaos of subsidences, into corridors, chambers, and halls. It takes a full century to produce five centimeters of petrification. And yet, look at this petrified waterfall—100 meters long and 20 meters high. Look at the elephant's ears hanging above us. Look where we have come to, far down now, and deep as we'll ever go.

"Jeremy," I say. "Imagine cavemen living in this wild place. Imagine thinking that the dome overhead was the first important sky and the sky that we know, the cup of heaven. That the sound of the water ceaselessly dripping was the sound of the wind going by."

"Eeww la la," he says. "They must have thought they lived in magic."

"I bet."

"They must have whispered."

"Sure."

"They must have been scared when they turned the lights out."

Perfect, I think. And there it is. The beginning of a story.

I take a deep breath. I fill my lungs with the fumes of the earth. I feel drops of mysterious mischievous rain burst on my head, wriggle toward my right earlobe. If I stood here long enough, I think, I'd be draped in a cloak of colored calcite. I'd be sealed inside the earth, in the dark, in a place 500,000 years old. A place that knows nothing of life on the other side, a place where nothing ever changes, not really, save the size and shape of all that glistens, and the echoes of fascinated boys.

The Things We'd Never Think Of

OURTH GRADE IS Mrs. Stanton, the things she teaches, the way she makes the kids crack up at the oddest things in the classroom. It is walking to Jeremy's school in the afternoons and walking the four blocks back home while Jeremy regales me with news from the playground, news from the classroom, news from the latest installment of Mrs. Stanton's Adventures, which seem to be in endless supply, spiraling in and out of the math, the English, the social studies, with pitched-to-real-children good humor.

On Tuesday afternoons, Jeremy waits for me in a classroom at the end of one wing, with thirteen other fourth-graders. I arrive with bags of food and colored pencils, with a dictionary and a thesaurus, workbooks. It's the Junior Great Books Club, for which I trained last spring. Be objective, the instructor instructed. Neutral. Measured. Rigorous with the Method. Keep your opinions to yourself. Remember your role as a guide.

I have, of course, never been neutral or measured in my entire life, but I have managed to get certified, and I am here because I want to be, because I believe in the idea of an after-school book club, believe in the power of talking books with kids, of edging all willing voyagers ever closer to parallel lives and fantastical lives, historic lives and serendipity. Closer, most of all, to one another. I like the notion of shattering the mythology that reading makes us more solitary creatures—of proving, indeed, how reading together can make us more socially aware, more political, more compassionate, more talented at conversation. It isn't about lessons here. No one gets a grade. It's about sitting around and talking books, in a classroom after school.

These fourteen kids are rambunctious kids, full of spunk and eager to make something of the time we have together. Though reserve and calm are called for by the "shared inquiry" philosophy of the Great Books Foundation, our Tuesdays most often erupt. Whether they read the stories at home alone or whether I read them aloud to the group, the kids react with heart and with head, and when they are angry or confused or joyous, I encourage them to say and be what they are, to emote, over pretzels and juice. If my certifying instructor could see me now and if I weren't volunteering, I'd likely be fired for all the hullabaloo. But when it comes to books and kids, I will argue, every time, for living the stories not just out loud, but loud.

So the kids read "Prot and Krot" and we talk and we inquire and we weigh and act it out. They read "The Man with the Wen" and "Thunder, Elephant, and Dorobo" and "Ali Baba and the Forty Thieves"—going a little too wild over the thieves, I suspect, for we are asked by a well-meaning teacher if we think we might have it in us to keep it down. It's late into the year before we plunge headlong into Kipling, an author, a dance number, I've been saving. I show them pictures of the life the author lived. I show them maps of where he traveled. I get a little rhythm going.

"Let us begin where it all begins," I say, when we turn our attention to his most rap-ripping of stories, "in the land of the Limpopo River, in the company of the Elephant's Child, his bulging, blackish, boot-sized nose, his powerful 'satiable curtiosity.

"Wait," I interrupt myself. "Just wait. What's this? *'Satiable curtiosity?*"

"Oh!" Fourteen hands are waving. Fourteen hands, like flags. "Oh! Oh! I know this one! I know!"

"'Satiable curtiosity"—I let Greg take the floor, watch his wire-rimmed glasses twinkle—"means an elephant who is very curious."

"But *nicely* curious," Michael adds, a smile beneath his spray of freckles. "He's very nice about his being so curious."

"'Satiably nicely curious," Alex takes his turn, his finger up, like a meticulous trial lawyer. "Don't forget the 'satiable part."

"But I don't get the 'satiable," I complain, to the kids. "What is it? Someone help me out here with this term."

"It's a Rudyard Kipling word." A chorus. "*You know.*" Twenty-eight separate eyes roll at me. I suppress my smile. I pretend *No*, I do not know. "Rudyard Kipling. He's the guy who makes his words *up*."

"Ah," I say, and for a while the noise chatters on as the kids place bets over definitions, then finally grab a dictionary. When they have satisfied themselves, I read on.

Oh, the places we go, the characters we meet. The questions the Elephant's Child asks himself into, the spankings he gets for being so thoroughly 'satiably curtiose. He wants to know what the Crocodile has for his dinner, and nobody's going to get in the way of an answer. I say, I read, *"Go to the banks of the great grey-green, greasy Limpopo River, all set about with fever-trees, and find out."* This is what the Kolokolo Bird tells the stump-nosed friend. So that the next day, I continue, *"when there was nothing left of the Equinoxes, because the Precession had pre-ceded according to precedent,*" the Elephant bundles up bananas and sugarcane and seventeen melons and heads off to discover the Crocodile's diet. The Elephant's Child is spanked, of course, he's dissuaded, he's even ridiculed. But nothing deters him, not even the fact that he doesn't himself know what a Crocodile looks like.

On he goes, east by north, through all those "promiscuous parts." Eventually he stumbles across the Bi-Coloured-Python-Rock-Snake, whose "scalesome, failsome" tail is also—and the kids find this so funny—used for spanking. Whenever we get to a part about the great grey-green, greasy Limpopo River, I hold my breath, and the kids sing the phrase, let it rip far, high, so loud. It starts sounding like hip-hop, or a parade. They are sitting down, I am standing up, but all of us are wriggling to Kipling's story. We know things are going to happen, and they do. We anticipate. We are answered. Whenever I can, I sneak a peek at the kids, these nine- and ten-year-olds who stay after school on Tuesdays to talk books, and not because they have to. Robert is blushing, and Steven purses his lips, and Dana's eyes, like her cheeks, are brightly dimpled. My own son can barely hold his laughter in, and the others aren't even trying. They are submerged in Kipling's tale, moving their bodies to the beat.

In the story, meanwhile, things just keep happening, growing wild. Pretty soon, we discover, the Elephant's Child is flat-out kneeling on the banks of the Limpopo River, begging the Crocodile to reveal his diet. "Oh no," the kids start saying, as I read this part. "Oh no!" They throw their hands against their eyes to fend off the fates. "Get away from the Crocodile," Samantha and Jillian warn. "He's going to eat YOU," Casey cautions, but it's too late. Because the Crocodile has his "musky, tusky" mouth on the Elephant Child's puny nose, and the tussle on the riverbank is growing heated. The Crocodile pulls one way, the Elephant's

Child pulls the other, they go back and forth and pull and pull, and it doesn't look good for the Elephant's Child.

"Pull harder," the kids are yelling, to the hero in the story. "Harder! Harder! Get yourself out of there!" Then: "Why'd he have to trust the Crocodile? Why did he have to be so 'satiably curtiose?'"

But I keep reading, and the kids keep urging, and I read, and the kids cheer, and soon enough Kipling brings the scalesome, flailsome-tailed snake to the rescue; the hero escapes his dire fate. When I get to this part, a victory roar goes up around the room. I look at the kids' faces; I smile. I take the tiniest break, a bit of melodrama, and then I read on as the Elephant's Child makes his way home, his nose now a finely stretched elephant-style trunk that is good for many things and also good for spankings. When I peer up at the end, the kids are swaying their own trunks—their arms stretched taut in front of them, their hands locked in a knot. They are swaying their trunks, and they are swaying in unison, fourteen Elephant's Children in a classroom, after school.

"Well that was a good one," Steven exhales, after I let pass a pause long and wide enough for things to settle. "That was good." I take it as a good sign, for Steven's hard to please.

"Yeah, I liked that," they all start at once. "I liked that one. We should do more like that. That was really, really good."

"Tell me," I say.

"What?"

"Tell me why. What makes Kipling's story so good?"

"Because of the made-up names!"

"Because anything could have happened!"

"Because of the great grey-green, greasy Limpopo River! Because of that!" Spontaneously then, they again grow themselves trunks and start swaying their appendages from side to side.

"Who else is as good as Kipling?" I want to know. "Who else makes you want to sing their tales?"

"*The Hobbit!*" Greg says.

"*Swiss Family Robinson!*" Steven offers.

"*The Phantom Tollbooth*," Jeremy says. "My number-one favorite. It's just so crazy. It just is." *Matilda* gets mentioned, and of course *Harry Potter*, and I ask the kids what these books have in common.

"Oh," Robert says, "it's how they take you anywhere. It's how they imagine these things you'd never think of."

"Did you ever read *The Time Machine?*" Steven wants to know. "Have you? My dad's read it to me."

"But have you read *The Phantom Tollbooth*," Jeremy insists, prevails. "It's just so crazy."

"Read *The Hobbit*," Greg says, his gestures earnest. "*The Hobbit*," he says. "You're gonna love it." I see Chris writing down titles on a page. I see Dana turning to Jillian to tell her about some book whose title, like its author, she's forgotten. I see Michael turning to Louis and Louis turning to Michael and Casey pulling a text out of his knapsack. I see an after-school classroom of rowdy, expressive, sometimes impossibly impulsive kids urging each other to read, declaring their views, setting themselves up for life, for that's what books do, that's why I am here: to witness the sound of a book-made moment. I let it go on. I wait many minutes. I finally break in with an idea.

"Hey," I say. "What do you say we all go Kipling? What if we all wrote a rap song using Kipling words and thoughts?"

"A rap song?"

"Yeah. You know. Full of crazy animals and ridiculous landscapes. Full of secret words like 'satiable and a sensational riverbank."

"The great grey-green, greasy . . ." They sing it out again, louder and louder and louder. I wait.

"Let's do as Robert says, okay?" I whisper, for I have learned that a whisper can, when all else fails, snatch their attention. "Let's imagine the things we'd never think of."

Imagine the things you'd never think of? The kids look at me, with my wild ideas. Jeremy stares, too, then shrugs. Whatever, Mom, he seems to say. *Whatever.*

"Hey," I say. "Yeah. That's exactly what I want. Imagine the things you'd never think of."

"You want a rap song about animals?"

"I do."

More noise. More buzz. More just slightly rebellious sighing as they lower their heads to their work.

Stars on the Ceiling

I HAVE A FRIEND who brings Jeremy stars one night in the cold, white dead of winter. They are the sort of stars that glow in the dark—paper stars with a sticky back that you press up to the ceiling. The package of stars is thin as a silver dollar, long and wide as a single page. They are nothing much, or they are something, depending on how you see them. What turns a child's head toward the stars? What makes any of us look beyond ourselves and see? How, in the end, does one nurture imagination?

My brother had an affinity for the night. For the spinning balls of gas with their radiant cores that he could pick out bare eyed, or with a succession of telescopes. My brother is like my writer friend, able to hold the science in his head, able to stretch out on the lawn and do the math of nuclear fusion, confront the facts of a dying sun, assign the colors of the stars to their probable temperatures. When we were kids, my brother had balsa-wood rocket ships suspended from his ceiling, planets dangling from transparent strings, Saturn bobbing merrily inside its rings. He had the pin-pricked maps of both hemispheres of the sky, a poster taped to the wall near his bed. The solar system was swirly color. There were some sixty moons. There was the Earth's own moon and its many crater scars, the story that those craters told about massive, ancient bombardments. My brother would lie in his room and just look at these things. Just lie there, looking up, astronomical thoughts in his head.

That was how our childhood was. We were given the room to imagine. This, at least, is what I remember—idling beneath the clouds and idling ankle high in creeks. Sitting with my uncle past-ing sequins onto Christmas cards. Standing beside my mother, pressing cookies out of dough. Going upstairs, or to the swing set, and writing poems into a book. And in the long, well-lit family room of that house in Delaware, my mother put on puppet shows, crouched behind the pinstriped couch, or my brother, sister, and I would sing to *The Music Man*, intoning loudest when we got to the song that spells *Trouble*. I had a mineral collection in the base-ment, just stones that I kept in a shoe box. I baby-sat the neigh-bors' cat when the neighbors went away, then managed three unexpected kittens. In summer twilight I was the kick-ball queen, slamming more home runs than any boy, and when it was really dark, my brother and I ran the hilly circle of that suburban neigh-borhood, timing each other with a stopwatch of sorts, as if we were working for Guinness. We lived in northern Canada for a while and hunted the aurora borealis. We spent a year in Boston, where we found and kept our own calico cat, skated on frozen ponds, lost and found our sister once inside a towering snowdrift. We returned to Delaware with the cat we named Colors. I doo-dled more poems in my books.

And all of us knew, all this time, that my brother had something of the rare about him, that he was smart in a way most people are not. I did not mind because he'd been born that way, just as he'd been born blue eyed and blond, a juggler and a whistler, angular and thin, without even trying. All he ever had to do to understand any scientific conundrum was to ask the question in the first place. The mathematics of theoretical phenomena performed their high jinks in his head. He wrote limericks and clever poems. He blew soap bubbles as large as the kitchen sink, and then explained how he did it.

I never felt threatened by his intelligence because he was simply who and where he was: two birth years ahead of me in human time and a citizen of a different cerebral planet. He liked to memorize pi to the three-hundredth decimal place: a convenient enough trick, I thought, for any backyard carnival. He could name all the stars in the sky; I showed this off to girlfriends. He played the clarinet and then the oboe and also the piano and also, who the hell could say just why, a pair of shiny cymbals. He thought fractals were fun and I thought watercoloring was, and we both liked to toss a ball across the lawn. We weren't competing against each other. He did what he did, he knew what he knew, and he was never sent away to Smart Kid Camp or Fractal Camp, not catered to by high-paid mentors, not rushed through the natural order of things and on to early college. He wasn't hovered over, I'm saying. His intelligence wasn't traded on. His childhood was not foreshortened, and his adulthood hasn't suffered.

My brother could have been a writer; he became a scientist instead. My friend could have been an astronomer; he's famous, now, for stories. Both of them, just slightly older than I, have held fast to their stars. They're still dazzled when night overtakes the day. They're still in possession of wonder. My brother takes his kids out in the middle of the night to see meteorites and moons. My friend tilts his daughter's chin toward Orion. These men are, I would like to suggest, who they are because of the time they've spent imagining.

We can make peace with the world through our imaginations, or we can locate the best of ourselves. We can formulate questions, tap our way toward knowing. We can intuit, empathize, appreciate, anticipate, find our grace. We can skate on a pond and think we're flying. We can drive in the dark with the music on and know the music's meaning. We can look at the stranger with the tear in her eye and imagine what she's thinking. We can clear a path between the actual and the dare, the real and the hoped-for, making something out of nothing, creating what did not exist before: fire from two sticks, say, or popcorn, or the Phoenician process called saponification, which yields a solid soap. How shall I raise my child? the young Katie Rommely asks her mother, in *A Tree Grows in Brooklyn*. Read your daughter a page from Shakespeare and the Bible every day, Katie's mother counsels. Raise her to believe in heaven. Buy a piece of land someday so that you might pass it on to her. And give her the gift of the imagination: "The child must have a secret world in which live things that never were."

Imagination, it is widely noted, is a form of intelligence. It is a form of inheritance as well. Without it, we're hardly human, and while it's impossible to know just when imagination first bloomed in man, it is tempting to agree with Jacob Bronowski in *The Ascent of Man* that the cave paintings one finds in Spain and southern France suggest something about the transcendent mind—the mind that opens itself to the lingering question What if?

> I think that the power we see expressed here for the first time is the power of anticipation: the forward-looking imagination. In these paintings the hunter was made familiar with dangers which he knew he had to face but to which he had not yet come. When the hunter was brought here into the secret dark and the light was suddenly flashed on the pictures, he saw the bison as he would have to face him, he saw the running deer,

he saw the turning boar. And he felt alone with them as he would in the hunt.

Bronowski's caveman has paused in the "secret dark." He has separated himself from the others. He's contemplating. He is breathing in and out, wheeling his thoughts forward, slowing things down in his mind, and here again is that reminder for us: Imagining takes time. We can't reasonably imagine inside the press of schedules, under the weight of obligation, within the claustrophobia of competition. We can't imagine if we're not given the space to spangle cards, shape cookie dough, chase the aurora borealis. We can't imagine if we're racing between here and there with a juice box and a bag of chips and a duffel bag stuffed with three costumes. We can't imagine if all we're aiming for is the bright blue ribbon or the polished trophy or the boasting rights at the Thanksgiving table. We can't imagine if we have no say in the way we spend our time.

I don't, at first, understand the thin pack of stars that my friend has brought my son. I can't guess their meaning. I don't know how to press them to the ceiling, how to assure the appropriate adjacencies between Orion, Cassiopeia, and Gemini, on the one hand, and Gemini, Ursa Major, and Cancer, on the other. My friend sends helpful notes about drawing quadrants on my suburban dome and reversing east and west, but I am at a loss and have nearly given up when Jeremy and I find ourselves snowed in one winter day.

In our tiny house, Jeremy has the single spacious room, if you don't count the ceiling height, which is constrained by a stingy roofline. He's also heir to the house's one true closet—a walk-in cupboard with a square configuration that lets him both stand tall and stretch out, if he wants to, and that also goes conveniently black when you firmly shut the door.

And so it is to this closet that we come on this snowy day to give birth to the glowy constellations. Still confused by east and west, I do my best to tape the templates to the ceiling in a respectable, vaguely true-to-nature way. When the taping is done I call out, officiously, for each self-adhering star. For Betelgeuse, for Alnitak, Saiph, Rigel, Mintaka, Bellatrix, Meissa, for the others with Greek symbols for names. I call for a star, and Jeremy peels it from the star page, sticks it to his index finger, touches it to mine, as if we are family with ET. Thereby starred, I turn and press my finger to the ceiling, adhering to the template. I press again, so that the star will stay put, and then I call out for the next star in the sky, and it goes on like this, through Orion and Ursa Major, through Ursa Minor, and then Leo, the great lion. In between constellations, I read Jeremy some facts about light-year distances and Greek mythology and Rigel, that blue supergiant and "one of the most luminous stars in the sky." I have nothing to offer beyond what I read in the books. This is something we are learning together, and we can only achieve the approximate.

Downstairs, meanwhile, the phone is ringing, and I am, as I always am, behind on deadlines. But we keep working. We keep putting our stars on the ceiling, even as the snow falls outside and the hours tick on and it becomes clear that Bill might get stranded in the city, that all the world is turning into a hush. We keep putting stars on our ceiling.

"Let's turn on the stars," Jeremy urges, after we have completed the installation work on the great lion.

"Now?" I ask him. We are only partway done. "Are you sure?"

"I'm sure," he says, before sprawling out, faceup, on the floor. "I'm ready."

"Close your eyes," I tell him.

He closes them.

"Cover them up with your hands."

He does.

"Okay," I say, "I'm turning out the lights. I'm shutting the door and making night." We count backwards—three, two, one. We take a breath. We open our eyes to the blaze of four constellations, the burning, believable glow of paper.

"Oh my," Jeremy, beside me, says.

"It's like Colorado," I say, "on a nowhere ranch."

"You mean when you were a kid?"

"Yeah, when I was a kid. I think I was ten. On vacation."

"Were your brother and sister there?"

"They were."

"Wait 'til Dad sees."

"Yeah, just wait."

Over the next several months, Jeremy will spend time in his darkened closet, looking up. He will troop his friends in to see. I will hear his closet door open and close and know the lights have been turned out, and on clear nights, outside in the breeze, I will see him look up and crane his neck skyward—locating Orion, hunting down a dipper, hoping the trailing lights of a plane are really the blaze of a meteorite. He won't be doing anything but looking. He won't be going anywhere except somewhere in his mind.

And then the paper stars will begin to fall from his sky. I'll find them, glowing, on Jeremy's socks, or deep inside his sheets. I'll try to fit them back into their ceiling constellations, but the stickiness will be gone; they'll be just paper then that glows. The constellations will grow incomplete—it will be blank where Meissa is supposed to be and naked gumminess instead of Algeiba. But none of that will matter, not really. The stars will have suggested something. They will have given a boy's room light.

The Velvet Beyond

A FTER THE SNOW thaws I take Jeremy to the local natural history museum, where we are both aware—I'm not sure why—of a profound absence of wind. A stiltedness. A stalemate. The resurrected bones of the *T. rex* don't beckon. The taxidermy seems overstuffed, weighed down. Even the rain forest display seems several disappointing steps removed from weather—some piped-in music, some photographs, some headdresses in lit glass boxes, but nothing that betrays the fact that the real rain forests of the world are perfectly primordial places.

"I sort of thought it would be different," Jeremy says, after we wind our way through Amazonia. "I always thought the rain forest would be interesting and rainy and, well, cool. I thought it would be cool."

"Well it *is* cool in real life," I tell him, looking to salvage this visit. "This is just a replica."

"I guess I'm more interested in the real than the replica," Jeremy says, after looking about the room again and scrunching up his nose.

"I can show you something real," I offer. "But we have to go upstairs."

"Is it better than the rain forest?"

"Yes, in fact. It is."

He shrugs. We find the stairs. We climb.

Our destiny is here, lying in wait. Jeremy and I take our places at its side. Beneath the low lights of his glass abode, it is a mummy, death defied. An elegant and elaborate art form. "Now this guy," I say to Jeremy, "is real. He tells a story."

"He's a little gross, Mom," Jeremy opines, after he studies the mummy's pinched nose, his shroud of skin, his stones for eyeballs, after he's walked the Egyptian's length and gotten a good look at its hands.

"Maybe he's gross," I say. "But he's real."

"I thought dying meant you disappeared."

"Dying doesn't mean *disappeared*," I say. "Dying means . . ." And here, recognizing the trap I have laid for myself in my eagerness to make something of the day, I subtly sidestep the matter by reciting the few things I know about mummies. I explain the Egyptians' love for the life they have lived along the fertile Nile: the crops, the sun, the horizon. "They didn't want to give it up," I tell Jeremy. "So they believed all life continued—that spirits thrived even after bodies died, that the spirits were hungry and thirsty, the works."

"That's odd." Jeremy is decidedly unconvinced.

"Look"—I gesture, directing his attention to a placard—"isn't this interesting? All the stuff they did to preserve the bodies?"

"What did the spirits need bodies for?" Jeremy asks.

"As a home base," I say. "A sort of shelter." Out of my league in the spiritual realm, I plunge deeper into the technicalities of mummy making—explain how the moist internal organs were removed and salted and kept in jars. How the mummy makers replaced the heart with a stone carved like a scarab and how they coated the body with a white powdery salt, inside and out, until it dried. Toward the end, I say, they rubbed the body with spices and palm wine. They filled its empty abdomen with more salt and more fresh spices. They painted the skin with a waterproofing resin, and then they wrapped the body up with loving care, tucking precious jewels into the long strips of cotton and linen and pouring resin across each layer so that nothing—not moisture, not bacteria, not time—could steal the body from earth.

"But, Mom," Jeremy says, still unmoved, "when you're gone, you're really gone."

"Is that how you see it?"

"I think so."

"Well, I'm not sure myself. Grandmom and Uncle Danny died a long time ago, but I always think they're around."

"They're in heaven."

"Isn't that being around?"

"Not in my beliefs."

"What are your beliefs?"

"That heaven is another place, and it isn't around here."

"Okay," I say. "I'm going to think about that. Maybe you'll think about it, too." We go home and I cook dinner while he plays.

A FEW DAYS later I am in the shower when I hear Jeremy calling to me from the hallway side of the door.

"Mom?"

"Yeah?" I turn off the water so that I can hear him. I stand there shivering in the dissipating steam, the shampoo a white cap on my head.

"You know how we saw the mummy?"

"Yeah."

"You know how you said to think?"

"Yeah?"

"Well, I've been thinking, Mom. I've been wondering what it's like to be dead."

"Uh-huh," I say. "Uh-huh." Oh, God.

"Well last night I did it."

"Did what?"

"I found out what it was like."

Silence.

"What I did was, I had a thought, and then I let it go until I was thinking about nothing."

"Then what?" I ask, not certain I really want this answer. Certain, in fact, that this time, in my quest on behalf of the imagination, I have taken things too far, disregarded the incontestable actuality that the imagination is not, by definition, always synonymous with good. There are dangers too. There are fantasies that should not go unchecked, delusions that can wreak damage, "fanciful thoughts," as one dictionary puts it, that stoke unacceptable behaviors. Everything has a dark side, and not all suggestible minds should be blithely suggested to. As a parent, one must be on the lookout, take precautions, think ahead.

But Jeremy, on the opposite side of the door, continues telling me about his thought, about this discovery he's made. "Then I closed my eyes and still thought nothing," Jeremy says. "Completely completely nothing. Then I opened my eyes, and I still had no thought. Do you understand? I was thinking nothing *and* my eyes were open."

"I understand."

"And then I knew what it was like."

"What it was *like*?"

"To be dead."

"Oh."

"And, Mom?"

"Yes, Jeremy?"

"It was peaceful."

Death as peaceful. I stand there shivering until I know he is gone, then turn the water back on. Slowly I work the lather from my hair—standing in the steaming suds and closing my eyes and imagining my kid imagining. He's gone as far toward *if* as a person can go, and he's returned with the promise of peace.

The Stuff of Memory

*W*HEN YOU READ a child a story, you are telling
him—with your groans and sighs, your high notes
and whispers, your rushing through and slowing
down—just what to pay attention to, just what you think a story is
and how language goes together. Remembering out loud is a lot
like reading out loud; it involves seduction, prodding, hinting. By
telling our children about our child selves, by transporting them
to the residual evidence of our past, we are saying, in so many
words: This is the stuff of memory. This is how memory works. We
are telling them, too, about the importance of childhood, about
how it carries forward, shapes us, sustains us later on.

So I, for my part, tell Jeremy about the weeks my child self
spent at the shore. I tell him how images leap from my memory
even now, bright and tantalizing as silverfish. I tell him about the
burgundy summer house with its white-pebble lawn and the birds
squawking on the edge of town and the bay crabs turning cardio-

vascular colors in a rattling kitchen pot and the girl in the red apron who scoops black-raspberry ice cream into a cone. I tell him how, in the caverns of my skull, whitecaps are being punished by a gray-green summer downpour and how Uncle Danny is beside me still, his trousers cuffed high as he wades in the eddies, his hand covering his mouth as he laughs. Stone Harbor, New Jersey, in August is ever present, I tell my son—the horseshoe crabs tangled with sea kelp on the shore and the glycerin blobs of deserted jellyfish and the crisply folded ten-dollar bill I once found, perched in the dune grass, like some exotic butterfly.

But what I return to most, for Jeremy's sake, is the final day of those Jersey vacations, each one of them repeated faithfully in my memory. I tell him about how the day would begin with my father setting out on his big-basketed bike and returning, a half hour later, with a box of sugary puffs. And how, after the baker's box was empty, my father, mother, brother, sister, and I would roam around the rental house, stripping it of us. We'd stack our clothes upon our beds, dig the quarters out of the couch, find all the little Bingo markers and restore them to the Bingo box. Wearing little but our faded bathing suits we worked, until there was nothing left to do but place the borrowed key upon the borrowed table and close the door behind us. We'd pile into the station wagon then and drive the two blocks to the beach, where we would empty the car of all that we needed for one final episode of summer.

Five towels, two beach chairs, one cooler, three buckets, four shovels, one green-and-yellow beach umbrella. Our bare feet burning on the sunbaked sand. My brother and sister already on their knees, at work on their sand tower, which was meant to last for all of time. They'd devised a proven trench-and-barricade system, a diversion for the flood tides, and my sister would take care of defenses, while my brother would sculpt the towers, while I would begin the backbreaking work of hauling damp and ungainly sand from one outpost to another. Tunnels, ramps, caves, secret passageways; by midafternoon the castle would be multicham-bered, firm.

But soon the tide would turn; the ocean always wins. Some mild tidal finger would reach the tower first and then, in an instant, the sea would be upon it, like a fist. We would throw our-selves against the aggressor like human ramparts, but the waves, gaining force, would have their way, and what might have been a monument would collapse upon itself. There was nothing left to do but fling our shovels down, race out into the sea, and rinse the sand from our crotches.

We waited, then, for the tide to wash back out, for the crowds to leave, for the lifeguards to descend from their wooden chairs and pull them toward the dunes. We waited until we owned the beach, until there was no one but us and the gulls and the peren-nial homeless guy and the lovers wrapped up in their towels. We waited until we heard my father declare that he'd found his first bivalve.

We couldn't go home, we could not leave Stone Harbor, until our father had had his tryst with the sunken clams. This is what I tell my son: that my own father was never happier than this, never any happier than when the five of us were on that beach together, pulling the clams out of the muck. It was our father—your grand-father—who taught us how to hunt clams with our toes, I say. Our father who showed us how to time the whitecaps before we dove and how to carry our trophy buckets back to shore, where we would dump the clams, in a clatter, across the sand. We'd crack open the shells and violently yank out the meat, and then we—the five of us—would stand in a circle and toss clam aperitifs to the spiraling, screaming gulls. This is the way we said good-bye. The way we promised to come back. The joy our father gave us, while the birds screamed down on us.

It's decades later now, but still I drive Jeremy to this beach and walk beside him on the shore. I tell him more about his grandfather and the clams, about the sand structures that succumbed, about the black-raspberry ice cream towered up on cones, about my mother and Uncle Danny. I take him up and down the streets—sometimes in winter, sometimes in summer, sometimes with Bill, sometimes with my brother—looking for the burgundy house with the pebbles. I comb the dunes with him in search of errant dollar bills. I point to the freckles on my cheeks and say, These are from Augusts in Stone Harbor.

Seashells and ten-dollar bills. Bingo chips and salted skin. A father's game in the afternoon. The hollered greed of gulls. You can't remember if you don't take care to see it in the first place. You won't remember if you don't love enough to learn to say good-bye.

"Love with all one's soul." This is the principle Vladimir Nabokov's mother lived by. "Now remember," she would tell her son—saying the words, as Nabokov writes in *Speak, Memory*, "in conspiratorial tones as she drew my attention to this or that loved thing in Vyra—a lark ascending the curds-and-whey sky of a dull spring day, heat lightning taking pictures of a distant line of trees in the night, the palette of maple leaves on brown sand, a small bird's cuneate footprints on new snow." A readily tantalized woman, as was her son, Nabokov's mother wanted him to see as she saw, to retain what he'd seen; she understood that memory is what remains after all else falls away. She understood, as Rilke understood, that there is, for the creator, "no poor, indifferent place." She understood, as Eudora Welty understood, that memory is bound up with seeing, and that discovery must be compounded with love, and that imagination ultimately depends on how well we've noted and preserved things.

We take our children to the places of our past. We sift the sand with them, we watch the gulls with them, we tell our stories to them, we ask them to listen. We take them to a favorite museum and show them the remembered case of butterflies. We take them to the mountains, to the footpaths between frozen rhododendron, to the abandoned toboggan chute. We take them to the old high school, the old neighborhood, the old things in the old boxes of their grandparents' attic. Look, listen, touch, feel. Take notice. Love—we say it again—and you'll remember.

And sometimes we don't need to go anywhere, or we can't, or we don't want to. Sometimes we simply sit with our children in the space of an afternoon trading memories for memories, questions for an answer. Weather often is the prompt—the snow that keeps us housebound or the rain that won't relent, and this summer it's a drought that gets Jeremy and me remembering. Alone each day until Bill comes home in our old AC-free house, we watch the grass turn starchy and the phlox gray out and wonder if the wind has evaporated.

While Jeremy tie-dyes his tongue with successive Popsicles, we sit in the kitchen imagining cool. The shadow beneath a butterfly's wings. Movie theaters. Waterfalls. Streams. Seville just after Christmas. The playhouse near the creek amidst the oak trees of a forest. Basements. We imagine, we remember basements. "If I were at Grandmom's," Jeremy says right now, "I would go into the basement and I would not come out."

"A good idea," I tell him.

"Yeah."

"What would you do there?"

"I'd explore things. I'd play." He begins to speak of the stuff of his grandmother's basement—the secret doors, the bulging closet, the paintings in gold frames, the Ping-Pong table with the flimsy net stacked high with kitchen things. Things, Jeremy mostly remembers—not smells, not feelings; he is ten. Then he recites the games that he has played in that basement—hide-and-seek and school and indoor basketball. Then he looks, with some expectation, toward me.

"My grandmother had a basement, too," I tell him, after a

pause, after I understand that it's up to me now to keep the conversation going.

"She did?"

"Yes she did."

"What kind?"

"The dark kind."

"And cool?"

"Very cool. And you had to be careful on the steps."

Jeremy gets up and retrieves another Popsicle. He sits back down and waits for more news of subterranean places.

And so I tell him what I remember, appeal to his senses. I tell him how my mother's mother's basement was no bigger than the footprint of her house, which was small the way city row houses are small, and big in the romantic way I used to see things. I tell him, in words I hope he will understand, about how my grandmother's basement taught me the meaning of the word *nostalgia* long before I harbored personal regrets. It contained what I could never know and promised what I longed to discover. There was hardly any room to stand, I say to Jeremy. There was a single snaking line of exposed floor, between all she'd saved and collected. There were things and smells everywhere else. My brother would sit at the heavy roll-top desk. My sister would straddle one of the countless boxes. I would stand in the back, near the dresses Grandmom had strung across a knotty stretch of rope, sifting through the chiffon and silk and cotton and wool, not to mention the dust in the creases. Every dress held a fraction of my grandmother's story, a chapter of her life, her simple glories. It held the way she'd laughed, the way she'd prayed, the way she'd spoken to herself when she'd brush her dark hair and fix her hat with a pearly pin. I would stand among her dresses, I tell Jeremy. I would stand willing myself to believe that my grandmother had lived a fairy-tale life.

Then we'd change places, I say. I would snake forward and my sister would snake back and my brother would move from the desk to the spindly chestnut chair. If we spoke to one another, I don't remember what we said, though I am confident that we would have whispered. If we displaced the flecks and bits and scraps from their messy, stacked-up stations, I am sure that we were careful to reassert them in their places: the photographs, the scrapbooks, Uncle Danny's old report cards, the autograph albums of movie stars that my mother had, as a star-struck girl, assembled. We respected our grandmother's things. They were to be respected. We understood that what she'd thought to save was sacred, not haphazard. We left some things untouched, on purpose, for the next visit.

"I like the foosball game at Grandmom's house," Jeremy tells me, in the midst of my remembering, bringing me back to present time. "And I like all the doors and where they go. And I like the corner where no one can find you. And I like the dartboard that no one else uses."

"Is that right?" I say.

"Yes. And did you know that Grandmom keeps Christmas presents down there, even in the summer?"

"Do you look at them?"

"Not really."

"Why?"

"Because I'd rather be surprised."

"Did you know that my grandmother liked to dance?"

"No."

"Oh yes," I say. "She did."

We sit remembering. Out loud, and then increasingly to ourselves. I don't know precisely where Jeremy's thoughts take him. I see him smiling through the hot haze, and I see him looking out the window, and sometimes I stop watching him because I am thinking about my brother, and how I wish that I could call him and ask what he remembers about that basement in Southwest

Philly. I would tell him of this nagging memory I have of Grandmom taking us down into that place for the first time—her skirt billowing out toward us and Grandpop on our heels, switching on the bare bulbs, saying there'd be meatballs for supper. I would tell him about my memory of the two of us descending between them, our own parents upstairs, rocking our sister, then just a baby, to her sleep. I would ask him if this memory is true, if I'd loved the details well enough to get the details right. Corroborating evidence. That's what I would ask my brother for. His memories complementing my own, giving them substance.

"It would be interesting to go to a dungeon," Jeremy interrupts my reverie. "To climb down narrow, dangerous steps."

"You've been to dungeons," I remind him.

"I know."

"In Italy. In Spain." I conjure up the specifics, trying to get him to do the same. I fill in his blank spaces with the particulars of geography, mood, and weather: You were on Dad's shoulders. You held your uncle's hand. I was afraid and stayed above, but you were brave and walked through the dark. And afterwards you had a Coke. And after that we took a train. And on and on, Jeremy offering up what he can remember, my questions pressing him for more. These memories are your possessions, I'm saying. These dungeons, with their chambers of cool.

Perseverance

I SEEMED TO THINK, when I was small, that all a writer needed was desire. Touch your pen to your chin, rest your head against a tree, put the pretty words on the pretty page, and that's the story. I don't know why I supposed it was so, but I thought posture spoke for talent.

It's a good thing that Jeremy has never made such simple-minded assumptions. My kid has always seemed to understand that every imaginative pursuit requires as many parts perseverance as dream. From the time he was able to lift one thing up and put another down, he has given himself "projects" to do—gone straight to them every afternoon, settling down as if to a job.

Sometimes these projects have been strictly organizational—put all the red cars on the plastic street map going south, and all the blue ones going north. Sometimes they have been statistical in nature—entailing tracking the results, for example, of a sporting event and filing the data into columns. Sometimes they have involved drawing up maps of imagined cityscapes, or creating and completing elaborate mazes, or "designing" computer software, a task that necessitates the sketching out of decision trees. For a while he was designing and producing his own magazines as if under deadline—rising early to create the covers, fashion the headlines, crayon and capture the news. Fragments of stories appeared through all of this—something about a shoe factory on Mars or a computerized spinning wheel, an idea about a snow child who lights the sky with stars or a town composed of chess pieces. But mostly Jeremy's interest has resided in getting things from A to B. His passion has resided in a study of sequence, all of which is prefatory to plot.

Lately Jeremy's fascination with how things go together has taken a new turn: He is learning, from his father, to draw comic strips. They have always had their private games and hobbies, Bill and Jeremy, but this fondness for comic strips can be traced to one thing: Jeremy's love for soccer. The international games that he follows on TV, the neighborhood league that he plays in, the soccer magazines that he subscribes to, the statistics he collects. How do you tell a story about soccer? How do you stop time, freeze it, show someone *the* crucial, telltale, game-determining moment? You draw it, frame by frame, or at least you can, and Jeremy has asked his dad to show him how.

So Bill takes a sheet of newsprint and fashions twenty two-inch perfect squares. He concocts an imaginary soccer game with imaginary players and drafts the action in so many split-second frames, Jeremy by his side watching and learning, me (who never did learn how to draw) entirely ancillary. The kitchen floor becomes a mess of paper and colored pens. The talk becomes yellow cards, red cards, probabilities, bicycle kicks, the referee who misses the call or the referee who unfairly favors this team over that.

Imagine a verisimilitude of players and teams, uniforms, referees. Imagine every play depicted so painstakingly well that, were you to cut out the frames and hold them like a pack of cards, then rifle through them with your thumb, you'd get the animation of a kick, a header, a goal, a dirty trick, a fine defensive play. Imagine the whole thing feeling just like TV—there are commercials, replays, halftime reports—and just like TV, there is an announcer calling the plays—or maybe two announcers. "Fancy footwork that," Jeremy says. Or, "And Luis Camines of Barcelona has the ball. He marks him . . . He reverses . . . He breaks free . . . He scoooooooooores!"

"Goal!" Bill answers. "Goal!" Both of them with their arms up now, in a big victorious V.

"It's the best play we've seen all season long in the Spanish Premiere League," Jeremy the announcer continues, his voice as low as his hormones oblige him. "Mallorca's Tino Aree is not one hundred percent, and Barcelona's hungry."

"There's still stoppage time," Bill interjects. "Mallorca can still make a play."

"Mallorca's down by two," Jeremy cautions. "But we'll be back after this commercial break."

And then off they go, into the commercial break, Jeremy taking the pen now, drawing up the ads, making Bill laugh with his inventions as he learns to stop action on the page. "Since when do they advertise birdhouses on TV?" Bill inquires of Jeremy now.

"On ESPN they advertise birdhouses," Jeremy says, his regular voice piping through. "I'm pretending here, Dad. We're making this up. Remember?"

I am just the shiver of a shadow at the edge of their bucket of felt-tipped pens, their oversized pad of paper, their floppy-socked feet. I am on my hands and knees chasing peas; they do not notice. I am swabbing at the mess of a solidified grape Popsicle drool; they do not care. I say, "Nice uniforms. Really. And what a goal." But my comments go unheeded. I wipe the table down, tie the green plastic ears of a trash bag, snatch at a kernel of corn that has fallen along the far kitchen wall. I ask who is winning, mostly out of politeness. Then I retreat upstairs.

AFTER BILL TEACHES Jeremy the mechanics of making comic strips, Jeremy begins to produce them on his own—his newest project. During the days in winter, when school is out and the yard is too sloppy to play in, he'll tolerate me and my suggestions for crafts (beaded key chains, poster paints), then rush off to the kitchen, grab his myriad statistics, and spill his pens all over the floor. Nothing is so seductive, just now, as the comic strips. Nothing is quite as sweet to him as the expression he knows his father will get when he comes home to a new stop-time story.

So today I am upstairs making the beds while Jeremy is downstairs, in the kitchen. I know what he is up to, with his sprawl of markers and newsprint, and I also know to leave him be, that a child left alone is not necessarily a lonely child. This is something that parents of an only child especially have to work to come to terms with—how to know the difference between lonely and alone, daydream and boredom; how to advance a suggestion at just the right time; how to let things perk and boil within a child's mind. You read a child's face; you know. You learn that his projects are his place to go, his way of exercising mind and soul, and you let him be, you let him call to you, you give him options, not directions. Where will these comic strips take Jeremy? What will he do with his knowledge about sequence? What do all the piles and piles of Jeremy's projects add up to, and where will we put them in this tiny, quiet house? I'm not quite sure, but just now, upstairs, I will not intercede.

Reading Alone

EADING ALONE BEGINS with the body, with settling in. Up, in the crook of the tree, or down, on the green grass below. On the floor beneath the ceiling fan, on the shore beside the retreating sea, over a plate of clam linguini, in the bathtub, late at night. Reading alone begins with settling in, with the posture of surrender.

You lie in the hammock that is strung up between two trees. You creep out onto the flat of an old tin roof or steal to the creek or settle onto an old raft at the beach. Our bodies change when we submit to books—our hearts beat that much quicker, or they quiet; our muscles lengthen out, or tense—and it is important, terribly important, that children learn the blessings of reading alone, for pleasure. They need to look at a page and hear its rhythms. They need to pause and think; they need to know their own agendas. They need to dwell—to flip back, sneak forward, anticipate, hold themselves in suspense for as long as they can stand it, slip away so that they can return. They need to have their own news to report. If one is never too old to be read aloud to, if nothing puts two people in the same mind space quite as well as that, one is also equally never too young to learn to love to read alone.

And so this winter, while I continue reading out loud to my son, continue walking around the edge of Jeremy's projects, I begin to lay the groundwork for him to read books on his own. I'm not speaking about mechanics; of course Jeremy can read alone. He can do his homework, finish his assignments, read whatever it is he needs to read. But need is not the point. Desire is. The capacity to fall so headlong into a book that one spends the night under the covers with a flashlight.

The more I urge Jeremy in this direction, however, the more he resists, the more questions he throws up as a defense. He tells me why he prefers that I read to him. He tells me the books he reads aren't as good as the ones I do. And then he says, "Well, here's the thing: I don't know how to sit when I read. I'm just not comfortable," he says. "I just don't get it."

He is sprawled across his bed with a book in hand. I am sitting beneath him, on the floor, with a magazine. I take a good look at the crooked line of him and his grave exasperation—at how he's propped up his head with one of his hands and smashed his book to the quilt with the other. Every time he needs to turn a page, he has to adjust all his weights, all his levers. He has to get use of both hands, turn the page, put the book back down, replant his elbow. A shadow falls across the words—he is blocking his own light—and now, in a melodramatic gesture designed to prove to me how tough all this is, he pitches his body to the floor, settles on his back, lifts his book above his head, and squints, as if looking at the sun. He looks at me and rolls his eyes. He half crab-crawls to a barren patch of wall and bangs his back against it, throwing his lean legs out straight.

"It's so much better when you read to me," he says with a sigh. "All I have to do when you read is wait for the story to come."

"Is that right?" I say.

"That's right," he says.

"Let me think about this one." I do.

Over the next several days I make it my business to understand the ergonomics of reading: the hands that hold; the fingers that turn; the spine that curves or straightens; the legs that must forget that they are construed of flesh and blood. At the neighborhood library, under the cover of a book, I watch the way a woman with flowy hair paces as she reads, walking up and down, up and down, stirring up a breeze in the stacks. I watch the way old men gather at the chest-high reference shelves and lay out their books, papers, and maps, like so many ministers at a pulpit. A boy with a leg-long cast hobbles in, finds a swath of natural light, and settles down, tossing his crutches to one side.

"There are plenty of ways to read," I report back to Jeremy that afternoon.

"Sure," he says. "Sure. But which one's comfortable?"

Slightly exasperated, I go to the basement and retrieve the book of Andre Kertesz photos. An unwitting inventor of the candid photograph, the Hungarian-born Kertesz had a way of documenting the unposed, the true. In his book there is a photo of an old woman in a hospital bed who holds a book like a prayer in both her hands. A man who stands before an outdoor cart of thrift-store-style books on New York City's Fourth Avenue—his face adorned with thick eyeglasses, his right hand holding a magnifying glass, his left palm cradling *Comradeship*, his nose breathless inches from the page. Readers in Washington Square backed up against trees, strewn over grass. An S-shaped woman in Paris, 1928, whose black skirt provides a contrast to the white pages on her lap.

"There are so many ways to read," I tell Jeremy. "So many, I can't count them."

"Sure," he rolls his eyes. "Yeah, sure."

I have failed, once again, to convince him.

So I ask my friends, my dear and treasured friends, whom, I realize, I have never noticed reading. I send them messages, urgent pleas, and while I wait for their replies, I read *The Enormous Egg* out loud and tell Jeremy I am still working on an answer.

Beth, my friend Susan messages back. *What a question you ask: How do I read? Well, I hardly ever sit when I read. I usually crawl under the covers in bed next to my reading lamp and hold the book above my head and prop my arms up with pillows. I can read like this for hours. And also, I really liked reading when I was pregnant, kicked back in a worn-out La-Z-Boy with a book propped up on my swelling stomach, and I also love to read in a really hot bath, but I'm always dropping the books into the bathwater and they swell up like little accordions. I had to stop doing that with library books.*

Jayne Anne, my novelist friend, my comrade in secrets, discloses a part of .herself I can instantly imagine, though I have never seen it for myself. *How I sit when I read?* she writes. *Preferably in bed, Dahn Center (Korean meditation), heated rice pillow on my stomach (that knotted flux of emotions), pillows behind, covers pulled up against the thirty-below wind-chill factor outside the windows — in the dark, just my light on, everyone else asleep. How I read more often? In the car, waiting at the train for my commuting teenager, just hoping that he's on the train, that my cell phone won't ring with a change of plans, that he has his gloves, his hat, even his coat. . . .*

You see? I say to Jeremy, a few days later. There's reading as a privilege, and reading as something we steal, and there're adjustments we make, on behalf of a story, sighs we don't sigh, because it's worth it. Reading is the occupation of the mind, the conundrum of the body, the thing that gets us from here to there, I tell him. You make your body work with a book, with light, because, in the end, it is worthwhile.

"I'd rather play soccer," Jeremy tells me. "Now *that's* comfortable."

"I'm not stopping you from playing soccer," I say. "But reading is fun, too. It really is."

"It hurts my arms."

"Well then we just haven't found the right position."

I read prone, Alex, my journalist friend, writes, to help out. *On our worn, mouse-infested couch. My head propped on a pillow, my legs covered by a blanket, often relying on whatever sunlight makes it through our windows. The other place I love to read is on planes and the El,* he explains. *It's the only time I read sitting up (not that I have a choice). On the El going downtown, I know enough to sit on the north side of the train; otherwise the sunlight hitting the moving train will make me nauseous.*

An hour or so later, Alex's notion is corroborated by another reading friend of mine, the man whose gift of paper stars is still partly clinging to Jeremy's closet ceiling. *I think my favorite place to read is on a train,* he writes. *I like to look up from time to time, to see the landscape passing in pace with the narrative.*

"Don't you love that?" I say to Jeremy, after I read him these notes. "This idea of reading on a train? I think you could do that, don't you? That sounds pretty easy. In fact, we've done it. We've read on a train."

"It's more fun looking through the windows while you read, Mom," Jeremy opines. "Or listening to you tell a story."

"Try to understand," I tell him, feeling frustrated. "Listen." And then I read him the message my friend Kate has sent, about how she sits (but only when her house is clean) in a low-slung Victorian rocking chair (green velvet upholstered, bought specifically for rocking babies and reading) in her bedroom, natural light from the north, a view of the bay that she's not looking at. I read him what Barbara wrote about folding one leg up under the other on a wide wicker kitchen chair, one hand fiddling with her hair, the other fiddling with the cover on the book—all of this going on until the day grows too dim and she takes her book to bed and lies in the light of a lamp. I tell him how two writer friends share a couch and a lamp when they read, and how Amy won't read a single word unless she's got her poodle on her lap.

"You can be an outlaw when you read," I tell Jeremy. "You can do it any way you want."

"Show me how."

"Show you how? You want me to show you how?" I think of all the times he's seen me reading, but I cede to the demand. Together we troop around the house while I demonstrate my favorite positions. In my office I throw myself horizontally over the puffy love seat, fit my neck upon one armrest, fling my feet over the other, and say, "Ta da. See how my knees come up to make a perfect support for the book? See how my head is upright so that I won't fall asleep? See how the window draws in the sun? See how there's quiet in here?"

"You're taller than me, Mom," Jeremy says, after he's tried it. "That couch just does not work for me."

"Okay." The love seat failing, I demonstrate my lunchtime position. Pull a chair to the kitchen table, plant my feet on the floor, balance a spoon in my right hand, take a book into the other. "My feet dangle," Jeremy says, after he's tried this out. "I'm not too comfortable here."

"Okay," I say. "Okay. Okay." And round and round our six-room house we go, trying out this couch, this chair, this rug, this stool, trying out the pace, the stand, the recline. Finally, we find ourselves back up in Jeremy's room, where there are soccer sheets and soccer quilts, a soccer rug, and soccer magazines. There is also (courtesy of my mother) a soccer beanbag chair, and Jeremy, dejected, flops down in this.

"Stay right where you are," I tell him. "Don't go anywhere." I trip over to his shelves and retrieve a book. A little paperback, light as a feather, called *Soccer Shock,* by Donna Jo Napoli. This book will have to appeal to him. It will have to fit in his hands. His body will have to feel at ease while it sinks into the beans.

He looks at me.

He rolls his eyes.

He turns one page, then another.

"How's that?" I say. "How's that? Okay?"

But I've lost him to the story.

Writing It Down

*A*T ELEVEN JEREMY begins to write with the single-mindedness that has always fueled his projects. He fashions comic tales and rapper lyrics, rhyming poems and complex novels. His casts are wide-ranging and multicultural. Plot, as opposed to mood, is paramount—a legacy, perhaps, of his fascination with sequence. Sometimes his characters come straight out of the cartoon strips he crafts. More often they come from that mysterious zone inside his head, that place beyond the veil of his dark eyes that keeps maturing and expanding. How he likes to write is on poster board, with Magic Markers or pencils. Where he likes to write is sitting across from me, at the sunlit kitchen table.

It all starts with *Marcus Wayne and the Robbers*, a sprawling, many-chaptered book that features a cat named Wood, a two-headed boy named Marcus, and an airplane pilot who is "mightified" (in Jeremy's words) with the power of X-ray vision. It progresses to *The Cartoon Studio*, which takes readers on a jaunt to an Argentinian animation company where all the managers are both power hungry and creatively stagnated. In *The Cartoon Studio*, Mrs. Elli Fasiz has a "thing" for young Paco Bellas. Chapter 1 opens with a mild debate and ends with an all-out scuffle.

Writing stretches Jeremy beyond the comic strips, gives him more room to maneuver, and as I watch him write, as I read his stories later, I catch glimpses of those parts of him that have been heretofore unexpressed or undeveloped. I learn what he thinks about when no one's looking. I learn where his ideas outpace his language, where he feels free to experiment, what pushes him back toward convention. I am startled, often. I feel a certain respect for his ingenuity, his determination, mostly, to translate imagination into words. It isn't always easy. In fact, it rarely is. But there he sits, pulling language across a page, not because it's been assigned but because this, in fact, has become his newest passion. This writing. These writing *projects*. "I don't want to be a writer, Mom," he warns me. "I just like to write and see what happens."

At the moment I am sitting here at this banged-up table with my books and things, and he's across from me, concentrating. *Once upon a time in San Francisco, California there lived a man named Phil Martyn,* he begins, and from this narrow, unthreatening starting place his story spills unself-consciously across the two-foot stretch of thick canary-colored poster paper. *Phil Martyn had graduated from college to be a news reporter,* it continues. *He had to go to Italy.* Now Jeremy gets stuck and pushes out his chair, stands, and walks in a circle around the table. He clasps his hands behind his back and hangs his head down low. He walks another circle or two, then holds up a cautionary hand in my direction in order to prevent an untimely interruption. "I've got the plot," he whispers. "I'm just looking for the words."

I whisper back, "Okay." I say, "Don't worry. I'm not talking." I do nothing to disturb his thoughts until he is back in his chair and once more writing. *When Phil got to Italy, people didn't know what he was doing there. He tried to give a report on the Leaning Tower of Pisa, but nothing interesting was happening. He knew he couldn't leave Italy that soon, so he took a fifteen minute train to Venice* . . . Now another walk around the table is required as Jeremy searches his mind for the next event in his hero's life. If I were done with my own work, I'd stand up and do noiseless things. Fold the laundry. Sort the socks. But I'm not done. I'm still sitting here, keeping my place on this side of my son's tender imagination.

Phil arrived at Venice after fifteen minutes and saw a pizza boat coming, he writes on. *The guy who drove the pizza boat delivered pizza to everyone. Phil decided to write about the pizza boat, but the people in Venice said that there's always a pizza boat that comes around.* Turning Martyn's thwarted reportorial opportunities over in his head, Jeremy stands and starts pacing, again, around the table, polishing the linoleum floor with his socks. He needs to know, after a little while, how to spell *Iran.* He stops, leans down, puts all four letters in their places. He circles the table yet again. I stand to make dinner. I sprinkle oregano, spoon out the white flour. My silence is the thing I do to keep this story going.

In time, Jeremy's Phil Martyn, the obedient news reporter, makes his way to Iran, where he hears the news that Americans are not allowed (or, as Jeremy writes it, *aloud*) in that country. It is headlines-making stuff, and Jeremy moves his character around the poster board, shuttling his hero off to China, where Martyn feels safe enough to file his Iranian report. *When Phil came back to San Francisco from China,* Jeremy finally, exuberantly, starts wrapping things up, *everyone had read the newspaper article about the president of Iran saying that no Americans are aloud in Iran. Phil got 1,000,000 dollars for his article. Phil gave* (and here Jeremy strikes that out and replaces it with *mailed) 250,000 dollars to China.*

I am surprised, when I stare at the poster board and find this ending. "He gave a quarter of his earnings from his first published story away?" I ask.

"Phil Martyn," Jeremy tells me, disappointed that I did not get this on my own, "gave his money away because China is poor and also because Phil Martyn didn't really need a million dollars."

What Does It Matter?

E WORKS, EXCLUSIVELY now, at the kitchen table, his own vast kingdom. Sometimes after school, sometimes late on Saturdays, sometimes early in the morning, sometimes with me sitting across from him with my own stash of things. Today I have notes and research cards spread on my side, Jeremy has colored pencils and markers on his, and I am losing myself in my own project. It takes me a moment to realize that Jeremy is doing nothing. That he is just sitting at the table, watching me.

"What's up?" I ask.

"I'm worried," he says.

"Why?" I say. "About what?" I look at his face, poised as it is on the cusp between childhood and adolescence.

"Mom," Jeremy says after a moment, "what I want to know is this: Is it only nonfiction that counts, that makes a difference?" He makes a gesture toward my side of things—my pile of the *New York Times*, my dictionary, my research notes. Nonfiction.

"Only nonfiction that *counts*?" I repeat the question. Counts? I wonder. *Counts?* Jeremy is not asking about personal satisfaction, not wondering whether he'd be happier with another genre. He has used the word *counts,* and I don't know what he means, what kind of answer my kid is looking for.

"I mean," he goes on, this fledgling plotter of crooked story lines, this near-master of the absurd, this writer of verve and imagination, "can only nonfiction change the world? Change people's hearts? Change what they believe?"

"Well," I say. "Well . . ." and my mind trips back to the conversation we had had not an hour ago—a conversation about a story that had run a few weeks before in the *New York Times Sunday Magazine.* The story was about the death of a doctor who'd been saving lives in Africa, and the story—its very existence coupled with the power of its prose—had produced in the *Times*'s readers such empathy and concern that the readers had responded with a spontaneous outpouring of funds for the doctor's family. "This is what a story can do," I'd told Jeremy. "This is why it matters that writers give their hearts to what they write. Because stories like this can change the world sometimes, or at least make a bad thing better."

"I'm right, aren't I," Jeremy says, because I haven't yet responded. "Only nonfiction counts, doesn't it? Only nonfiction can make good things happen for other people."

"Well," I say, and I am not stalling, I'm merely looking for the words, but he cuts me off with a sigh before I've produced a single fleck of counterevidence.

"Yeah," Jeremy says. "That's what I figured."

"No," I say. "Wait a minute. . . ."

But he has already set his story aside and he's packing up his things for school. We get in the car. I drive the familiar roads. We talk about lunch money and math, stay clear of his question. We pull into the school's drive. He opens the door then closes the door, and after that he's gone.

Back at the house, I walk the downstairs mulling over Jeremy's question and kicking myself for my nonanswer. Yes, I should have said, fiction too can change a heart. Not all the time, but sometimes. Fiction can provoke kindness, change a point of view, make someone out there care. Your fiction has the capacity to affect another, I should have said. The best of fiction always does.

In Jeremy's absence, I retreat to my long wall of double-stacked books, my own private version of a trophy shelf. On bad or unproductive days, on days in which I'm feeling dramatically unworthy, I tend to gravitate to this wall, to try to counter my moodiness by remembering what I've read. At least you've read James Agee and Faulkner, I'll tell myself on dispiriting days. At least you've read Willa Cather and Eudora Welty and Alice Munro and Wallace Stegner and Elias Canetti and John Updike. At least you've read, I'll say, as I drag my finger down the spines of books. You can't be all bad if you've read. Though reading, of course, doesn't make you good either. It just gives you more things to consider.

I pull some favorite volumes to the floor and sit among them. I think about all the ways I've been rescued by characters who only ever lived on paper. Rescued from loneliness. Rescued from boredom. Rescued from sleeplessness and sickness, tedium and trials. I think of all the sympathies fiction has generated in me, all the sudden swells of terror, heartbreak, hope, and calm that have come my way through novels, tainted my politics, held me somehow accountable to an idea or a dream, made me want to do something more extravagantly useful with my life. Fiction changes the world, one willing reader at a time. And this is what I should have said.

I have William Maxwell's *So Long, See You Tomorrow* on my lap. I crack it open to a favorite line—"There is a limit, surely, to what one can demand of one's adolescent self"—and think about atonement as it is projected by this novel. I reach for Paul Horgan's *The Richard Trilogy* and think of how often I have taken sanctuary there. I pick up Alice McDermott's *Charming Billy* and Chang-rae Lee's *A Gesture Life* and Patricia Sagastizábal's *A Secret for Julia* and Olaf Olafsson's *The Journey Home* and Bernhard Schlink's *The Reader* and Seamus Deane's *Reading in the Dark*—all books about the consequences of lies and obfuscation—and I try to imagine what the world would be if we were ruled by people who kept such books on their shelves and took their cautions from them—who read, as part of their daily regimen, passages like this one from *Trilogy*:

> "In every life, Richard, there is something, great or small, to be ashamed of," said my father, with more force than necessary, and with reference to a concern unknown to me then; for we were simply conversing in general. But the priest hidden in every Irishman was being eloquent in him, and his eyes flashed even as he smiled with scowling charm. "Just as there is something noble. Never fail to be ashamed of the first, and never take credit for the second. You'll remember this. . . ." He paused. Then, "I've tried to."

Wouldn't that change the world? Or, at the very least, couldn't it? Doesn't it already, sometimes, and isn't that what I should have said to my son—explicitly, and not by implication? Because we all need to believe that what we're doing *counts*. Because *counts* is different from makes us famous, makes us rich, makes us more important. *Counts* is about making a contribution—a real one—and sometimes fiction does.

I leave the books where they are and return to the kitchen, where the stuff of Jeremy's novels and poems lies everywhere about. In the advancing morning light, I reread Jeremy's newest tale of adventure and magic, his sly asides, his inside jokes, his puns. I study his crowded character charts and the dialogue he snuggles into quart-sized quotation marks. I look at what he has imagined, then transformed with words, and I know that even if there is nothing grandiose, nothing Nobel Prize winning here, it is—absolutely—the work of one who hopes to change the world, or at least, who hopes that the world is capable of being shifted, tendered, rearranged, awakened by all that finally transcends the news. We need courage like his, I think, in the face of the facts. We need the lyric irony, the redemptive power, the rescue, the light, the heart, the grace of stories that are born in one's head. We need fiction, and even more than that, we need the staunch, heroic, searching young souls who sit with Magic Markers and poster board and do their best to write it.

The First Summer Workshop

*B*UT NO MATTER what I tell Jeremy later that day, the fact is that few people beyond his father and me take any interest in his stories. The one time Jeremy summoned his courage to take one of his "novels" to school, the teacher who he hoped would read it couldn't find the time. The one time he asked a neighborhood friend if he wanted to hear a made-up story, the boy just shrugged. There's no after-school book club offered by his fine middle school. No literary magazine. Singers, instrumentalists, athletes, the "gifted" are extended every imaginable opportunity—mentors who take an interest, programs that highlight talents, uniforms that establish hierarchies, before-school and after-school initiatives in which friendships are made and self-esteem polished.

But Jeremy is writing stories, and just now there's no one but his father and me for him to share them with. He has asked me if what he's doing *counts*. I want to make certain that it does—not just for him, but for others. I want kids to be able to imagine out loud and to have a good time when they do, and this is what prompts me to reconvene the kids with whom I'd danced to Kipling. I've missed them, for one thing, and it has become important to me that Jeremy see the effect of his work on others, that he hear how other kids imagine, that we establish a community around stories not just listened to, but written.

The parents, for their part, don't seem to mind. Some even let me conduct the workshop in their homes. I will, I decide, knit together a program suited to firefly nights, bowls of popcorn, a mishmash of chairs, kids on summer break.

In the days leading up to this summer session, I sit in my office, remembering teachers: The second-grade teacher, who kept track of me through my family's many moves. The high-school teachers who helped me think I could dance with words. The college professors who caught me in the snare of their own intellectual passions. The librarian at my son's elementary school, whose love of books and goodness of heart are transparent and effecting. I think about my teaching friend who buys a book for every graduating student, about my teaching neighbor, Jane, who respects her students with the same conviction that she respects the rest of us. What qualifies a person to teach? I wonder. How much does one have to know before one returns what she has tried to learn herself, through accident, experiment, or application?

What I come to think, as I prepare, is that teaching is like parenting, at least in some regards. Like parenting, teaching calls for an empathetic imagination, the patience for second chances. It requires the discipline of a framework and the willingness to step outside that framework if—in that room, in that mood, in that moment—another approach seems justified. Teaching is not so much about passing something on as it is about being open to the question, not so much about distillation or summary, but about widening the scope of inquiry. Teaching writing largely concerns teaching reading, I think, and teaching reading is about urging another to know her own mind, to answer, for herself, how the book made her feel, how the dream drew her in, how the detail resonated, how the conceit and structure and language and plot did or did not satisfy. I know enough not to insist that the kids love the books I'll bring to them. I am inclined, instead, to help them understand why they love the books they love, and how that fondness, that preference, that *bent toward something* gets translated into writing.

My central objective, then, is principally the same as it was during those Tuesday afternoons: I want the kids to fall lavishly for books. But this time I also want to get the kids thinking about the work that authors do to create mood, establish place, construe shock endings, philosophize. I want the kids to reflect on all that happens behind the page, inside the mind of the writer.

We gather in the screened-in porch of two brothers' home for our first summer session. Sitting with the kids on an assortment of indoor/outdoor chairs, I raise the specter of irony. I read the definition of irony from *The Concise Oxford Dictionary of Literary Terms* and make a fuss over each big word: *subtly, humorous, perception, inconsistency*. Tell me what those words mean apart, I say, and tell me what it means if you string them all together. The kids give it everything they've got, and then we move on to the real world.

"So," I say, "What's ironic? What's ironic in your lives?"

"It's ironic that I'm here," says one kid. "Because actually I love baseball."

"It's ironic that Alex is holding the bowl of popcorn since I know he doesn't really want it," said another, as he leans across the room to grab a handful of the stuff.

"It's ironic that my mother is talking like a teacher," Jeremy says, and the kids look at me and companionably snigger.

"So you've got it," I say. "You've got ironic. And ironic is part of what we'll do tonight."

"Be ironic?" one of them asks.

"Yes."

"All night?" another chiming in.

"At least some of it."

"Well isn't that ironic?" Three kids say at once, then laugh.

The plan is to read "The Invisible Child," by Tove Jansson, a single tale from a larger collection titled *Tales from Moomin Valley*. In the story the characters are a clan of former wretched trolls who have been transformed (before we meet them) into something more like sweet hippopotami. As the story opens, the Moomin family is sorting through a mushroom harvest when a neighbor, Too-Ticky, stops by with an invisible friend named Ninny. Ninny, we learn, has been rendered invisible by an unfortunate encounter with an "ironical" woman. When Moomintroll wants to know what *ironical* is, Too-Ticky explains in this manner:

> "Well, imagine that you slip on a rotten mushroom and sit down on the basket of newly picked ones," Too-Ticky said. "The natural thing for your mother would be to be angry. But no, she isn't. Instead she says, very coldly: 'I understand that's your idea of a graceful dance, but I'd thank you not to do it in people's food.' Something like that."
>
> "How unpleasant," Moomintroll said.
>
> "Yes, isn't it," replied Too-Ticky. "This was the way this lady used to talk. She was ironic all day long every day, and finally the kid started to turn pale and fade around the edges, and less and less was seen of her. Last Friday, one couldn't catch sight of her at all. The lady gave her away to me and said she really couldn't take care of relatives she couldn't even see."
>
> "And what did you do to the lady?" My asked with bulging eyes. "Did you bash her head?"
>
> "That's of no use with the ironic sort," Too-Ticky said. "I

took Ninny home with me, of course. And now I've brought her here for you to make her visible again."

The rest of the story is devoted to first locating (thank heaven for silver bells strung around necks) and then making visible this poor irony-blasted Ninny. Bit by bit, parts of Ninny come into view only to disappear again in proportion to irony and kindness.

But the point for me and the kids is to identify every irony we hear inside this strange and wonderful story. "When you hear something ironical, give a shout," I say, and it isn't long before the game becomes something of a harmless competition, with the kids keeping scorecards on their laps.

At every imaginable juncture, we're talking irony, and every time the ironic blossoms in the tale I try to go a little deeper, to get the kids to think about the author at work. Why is Tove Jansson doing what she is doing? How is she using irony to move the plot? And how would the kids deploy the ironic if they were the ones writing the story? What ironic episodes would they engineer for this clan of former trolls?

When you're the author, you decide. This is the point I am making. When you're the author, you can use irony any way you want. In Jansson's case, she goes so far as to suggest that Ninny isn't completely, visibly cured until she becomes ironical herself. Which is, of course, a strictly ironic trick ending that leads me to the gate of my next lesson.

"All right," I say, "so you know what irony is, and you know a little bit about how to use it. Your next assignment is to pretend that you're a writer—call yourselves O. Henry—who has written a funny, heckling tale about a kidnapping gone crazy in Alabama. My job is to walk you up to the cliff edge of this story, and then I'm going to stop. You're going to take over right at that cliff edge and write the ending to the tale. The only thing I ask of you is that you craft some kind of trick—that you surprise the rest of us with what you do."

All of a sudden quiet in their chairs, their bowl of popcorn empty, the kids sit back while I read aloud about the loudmouthed boy who has a too fine time upon the occasion of his own kidnapping, in "The Ransom of Red Chief." The boy keeps terrorizing the men who are supposed to be terrorizing him. He seems far too delighted to be along for the ride. He talks and talks, without an apparent care for logic. He goes ridiculously on, spieling his way through nonsense: "Are there any real Indians in these woods? I want some more gravy. Does the trees moving make the wind blow? We had five puppies. What makes your nose red, Hank? My father has lots of money." And so on.

Maybe, the kidnappers come to think, this rowdy kid isn't the sort of kid a father would miss. Maybe this kidnapping is going nowhere. Maybe it's time to write the kid's father a letter.

Here at last we reach the promised turning point—the kidnappers are about to sit down and pen a ransom note—and here is where the kids take over from O. Henry. "You can do whatever you want," I remind them. "So long as you surprise us." I give them fifteen minutes and refill the popcorn bowl. A few of the boys slap their papers on another's back to write. Two of the girls lean against each other as they share a clipboard on the floor.

By the time the parents return to collect their kids, we've heard a dozen different ransom letters, some of them pleading, some of them smug, at least one of them signed by the boy himself, who begged his father to let him continue his adventure. When the jam session is done, I finish reading O. Henry's version, showing the kids how O. Henry had turned the tables on his own tale with a clever ransom note and an even more clever response on the part of the miscreant's father.

"You mean the father wouldn't take the son back unless the kidnappers paid him two hundred and fifty dollars?" one of the girls says, smiling.

"That's right," I say.

"Well isn't that ironic?" the kids say, together.

"Very," I say. "Very ironic."

ONE EVENING DURING most weeks this summer the kids and I gather to expand our understanding of what tools writers use and how they use them. We read "Sindbad the Sailor" to jump-start a conversation about alternate realities, and then—following a small detour during which each boy and girl tells me an alternative version of their actual day—we construct alternate reality game boards, making up the rules as we go along, so that, for example, one game-designing team determines that every odd space on the board cannot be passed until the player answers a question from a deck of cards that they've created.

The next week, the kids the read Armstrong Sperry classic *Call It Courage* at home, and then we sit in the basement of a generous parent's house and talk about character development and point of view before we finish up with an exercise in which the kids take the book's haunting final scene and rewrite it as if they were reporting the story on behalf of the *Times*. We use *The Family Under the Bridge* to talk about how authors evoke place, then follow that conversation with the development of rhyming descriptive poems about the kids' favorite hidden places. We use "Rikki-Tikki-Tavi" to talk about adjectives and adverbs, and every time either one of those word forms appears in the text, the kids write it down, make long curvy lists, and write their own poems with the "found" language. And then one night I read parts of *The Adventures of Huckleberry Finn* aloud—outside and under the stars. We talk about how dialect shapes and propels character—how the *how* of Jim's talk tells you about *who* he is—then we go to the next obvious step, writing and performing dialect-driven pieces, filling the night with exotic chatter.

As the end of summer comes, we convene at my own house,

where the plan is to discuss *The Call of the Wild*, which I've asked the kids to read at home. It's a grown-up book, and I know the talk will take us places—that we'll be getting into the stuff of theme and symbol, good and evil, violence and nature. I don't have a writing exercise prepared for this last night. Instead, I have asked the kids to be ready to think like critics, to use all the terms and ideas we've been sorting through and apply them to the story of Buck as well as to the story behind the story.

I have an old rocking chair that was bought just before Jeremy was born. I plunk it down in the middle of my family room and sit on it while the kids lie sprawled on the floor around me—passing bowls of snacks, licking the salt off their fingers. Outside it is dark but the air has not cooled, and in a far corner of the room, a floor fan hums. Everyone has come for the final night. Everyone wants to be here. *The Call of the Wild* is that kind of book. That kind of fierce, soulful, unwavering book that breaks the rules and is excessive and yet exerts its power. "You are the critics tonight," I tell the kids. "This is your own conversation."

To get things going I read from an early scene in which Buck, once a domestic dog, asserts his right to survive in the wild place to which he's been brutally transplanted:

This first theft marked Buck as fit to survive in the hostile Northland environment. It marked his adaptability, his capacity to adjust himself to changing conditions, the lack of which would have meant swift and terrible death. It marked, further, the decay or going to pieces of his moral nature, a vain thing and a handicap in the ruthless struggle for existence. . . .

. . . He did not steal for the joy of it, but because of the clamor of his stomach. He did not rob openly, but stole secretly and cunningly, out of respect for club and fang. In short, the things he did were done because it was easier to do them than not to do them.

Like so much of Jack London's classic, this passage is fraught with moral assertions that run counter to the code of the civilized world. Are value judgments about good and evil irrelevant in the wild? I ask the kids. How does London make Buck's dilemma real to us? And is Buck's dilemma really a dilemma for Buck, or an opportunity for the dog to become his true wolfish self? Tell me what you discover about character, dialect, place, adverbs, adjectives. Tell me if you think an irony is at work.

Passage by passage we work our way through *The Call of the Wild*, as Buck evolves from a dog in shock to a dog surviving to a dog who fights for mastery—with cunning and imagination and without mercy. Buck is also a dog who chooses to love a man named John Thornton, but always on his own terms: "He was a thing of the wild, come in from the wild to sit by John Thornton's fire, rather than a dog of the soft Southland stamped with the marks of generations of civilization. Because of his very great love, he could not steal from this man, but from any other man, in any other camp, he did not hesitate an instant. . . ." But that isn't all that Buck becomes. Buck finally becomes wilderness itself. "Man and the claims of man no longer bound him."

With humbling care and conscience, the kids sift through the story as the fan struggles to keep the room cool. Unafraid to assert, they are equally unconcerned about standing alone with their opinions. They make their claims and steadfastly hold to them as they take the side of man or beast or fate. Faces get red, hands slap the floor, and there are times when everyone is talking at once so loudly that I on my rocker have to bring a quiet to things, untangle the arguments, restate the debate in new terms. But most of the time the kids forget I am here. Most of the time, it doesn't matter.

It is late when the parents begin to collect on my front stoop. I hear them out there, but don't think the kids do. In my rocking chair above the grand debate, I imagine the parents tolerating the bugs that will be thrumming in the porch light, checking their watches, making talk. I imagine them trying to assuage any worries about so much excessive noise at what was advertised as a book and writing club. Finally one of the fathers opens the door on his own, walks down the hall and into the room, and announces rather hopefully, "Aren't we ready to call it quits?" He looks at me, parent to parent. And then I look down at the kids.

We're just getting started, I think. We're just starting to creep behind the words on the page. We're just beginning to find out that this *counts*, that we can be changed by what we read and that we can change others by what we write. But the truth is, this summer of books is over; it is time to say good-bye. Out into the night with their parents the kids go—still noisy, still chattering, still trying to persuade themselves of something. I stand on the lawn and wave good-bye, turn off the porch light, slowly weave back inside. When I turn back around, the cars are gone; the street is absolutely quiet.

In the house I find Jeremy on the old rocking chair, creaking back and forth, catching the fan's wind in his hair. Deflated balloons are at his feet. Pens a few kids left behind are scattered about, a few greasy popcorn bowls litter the floor. Jeremy is just sitting in the chair, rocking back and forth, with an expression on his face that I have not seen before.

"We can always do *White Fang* next summer," he says. "Right, Mom? *White Fang*? Next summer?"

"Is that what you want?" I ask, leaning down to collect the bowls.

"Maybe," he says. "*White Fang* could be good. Unless there's something better."

"We'll figure it out when we get there, okay?"

"Yeah. I guess. There are so many books. So many really good ones."

"Which you can read on your own through the school year, you know."

"I know. But it's funner getting together."

Wherever They Are Going

*I*T IS ABOUT time when we begin, about the math on the face of a clock. Find your way and keep a promise. It is about that as well.

"Okay, Jeremy," I say. "Meet me at the deer tongue on the north side of the pond in sixteen minutes, starting from . . . now."

"Sure," he says. "Sixteen minutes." Screwing the gargantuan watch around his wrist until it sits just right, moving his lips as he whisper-calculates, then fleeing cartoonishly quick: Roadrunner. I am left beneath the white oaks and tulip poplars of the local arboretum—in that modest forest preserve, where the trees stand silver necklaced with their common and Latin names, and the plants squat unpretentiously beside weatherproofed placards. I lumber east, toward the pond. Jeremy sprints west laughing, sneakers slapping, so as to give the charge a challenge.

It is almost fall. All writing club friends and other known adolescents are at the beach or at day camp for one last fling at freedom. We are alone, and this arboretum has become the site of a game we've played throughout summer. I'd meander Azalea Hill. Jeremy would sprint the inclined zags of Woodland Trail. I'd hear his feet, then I wouldn't hear them. Hear him breathing; nothing more. I'd check my watch and walk and read, I would consider: Strawberry Bush. Jack in the Pulpit. Bleeding Heart. And every week the green things changed—vamped, peaked, receded, hung their heads—and I took notice of their names. Cinnamon Fern and Colt's Foot. Spring Beauty. Dwarf-Crested Iris. Blue Phlox, Bellflower, Chinese Witch Hazel, Shining Sumac, Skunk Cabbage, not to mention the hydrangea. Twelve minutes. Fourteen minutes. Sixteen minutes. My son. On the north side of the pond beside the deer tongue, shoes untied.

"So," he'd say.

"So," I'd answer.

"Twenty-two minutes at the circle of azaleas." His call to make, and he would make it, and then, like Dakota weather, he'd be gone. I was teaching him to respect the appointments he'd be making. Teaching him north, south, east, west, white oaks, and tulip poplar. I was teaching him, I told myself, to go out into the world and then come back. But I wasn't teaching him, of course. I was teaching me. To start stepping back and giving him more room to go wherever he is going.

The azaleas are virulent at the local arboretum. The rhododendrons, for their part, can grow terribly thirsty, their leaves going thin as puppy ears when the rain has kept them waiting. Male cardinals are tame on branches of dogwood and Empress trees are awfully moody and blue foam flowers evaporate beneath white pine, tent moths cage the elderberry, cattails blow themselves to bits. You can circle the pond and then zag Woodlands Trail and head down, then up to Elisabeth's Walk in the space of any given measure.

"Sit with me," I say to my blushing, breathless son. "I'm an old woman. I need my rest."

"You sit," he says. "I'll come to you. In thirteen minutes."

This is the point of that arboretum, as we have construed it. These are the promises we keep. This is how I teach time and math and adolescence, the only way I know to teach it. Be there then, I say, and Jeremy is. You can go if you come back. And over and over, he goes off. And then comes sprinting back.

This hazy, lonely day of summer the skies want to rain but cannot find the gumption. It is cool until you move an inch, and then the sweat comes freely. "We're going to the trees," I told Jeremy, as soon as he got out of bed earlier.

"All right," he said. "For how long?"

"For as long as you want," I told him. "Or until it rains. We'll see. Whatever."

I proceed up Azalea Hill, toward Woodlands Trail, then down around the pond. I can hear Jeremy's footsteps, and then they are gone. We have forgotten, for once, to establish a rendezvous—I had not extracted any promise, and he had not offered one. The cattails are imploded. The ducks are missing from the pond. The hibiscus is still braving red in a grove of mixed witch hazel. I walk in circles, in and out of oblique angles, ruined sun. I feel the want of rain above, hear the rattling of acorns.

What lies ahead? True adolescence. The notorious teen years. A child breaking free from childhood. What will those years be like? I do not know. Will I have wisdom to give? This is the story not yet written. For parenting, I keep learning, is a stereometric enterprise: We aspire to wisdom in the here-and-now by applying the lessons of our private pasts and gauging the unpredictable future. We do what we can—dodging the temptation to take credit for what seems to work out right, accepting that we likely played some role in whatever goes awry. We aren't our children, and our children are not us, and yet it is our responsibility to give them the very best of us, and then to trust them with all the messiness and sweetness and life that will inevitably follow and that we as parents can do little to effect.

I, for my part, have been emphasizing literature and the imagination. Reading and writing, and the conversations those things spark. I have been focusing on giving Jeremy the tools I think any person needs to read the world, to respond to it, to make a positive difference. I doubt Jeremy will grow up to be an author. I'm not sure that I'd want him to be. But I am hoping—even, I admit, idealistically hoping—that the conversations we're having now about why characters (people) do the things they do and how characters (people) evolve, affect, forgive, transcend, struggle, again transcend, lead, follow, and finally let go will be carried forward into whatever he chooses to do as the man he will become. I am hoping that the time we've spent on the imagination will enable him to foresee the consequences of actions not yet taken. I am hoping that it will reinforce a compassionate heart. I am hoping that it will steel him for the hardest times, by giving him faith in another, better day. I am hoping that all this imagining will help Jeremy to know himself in ways I did not know myself until it was, sometimes, too late. I am hoping, a mother's simple dream, that it deepens his happiness.

Other parents and children find their place with music. Others find it with a ball or in the kitchen or at the pottery wheel in the basement. Or they introduce their daughters to fencing, or they encourage their son to take care of an anguished dog. The important thing for us parents, it seems to me, is that we share what we know and love and believe in for the sake of our child's wholeness and well-being. To help develop, in our children, a healthy sense of self, an abundant curiosity, a proclivity for dreams, a talent for seeing that is separate from—and never defined by—the number of trophies that might result from such full-bodied living. The important thing is to help develop a person, and that is different from developing a vehicle for our own parental pride. At the end of the day, listening is just as critical as leading. At the end of the day, we must take our cues from them.

In this family we have—in so many ways, for so many reasons—opted out of the competition that seems to define so much of modern life, that Woody Allen has, indeed, been spoofing now for years. We have not hired a private track coach, as we know others have done, to give our son a shot at a place on the afterschool team. We have not sent him off to a string of selective camps with the sole purpose of bolstering his resume. We have not continuously looked ahead to SAT scores and college admissions, outfitting him with what he'll surely need. We haven't pushed him up to the highest math tier even though we all suppose that, in a haze of anxiety, he could get the work done. We have not presumed to know what he wants to be, but have waited for him to tell us.

This has left us, as I have mentioned, on the edge of things. It has left us outside the societies that form around shared ambitions. It has left him with a less quantifiable future and certainly it has opened us to questions. You're hurting your son, people have said. It's about getting into Harvard, others have insisted. It's about winning, always about that.

In the scheme of some things, these parents are right. It's Darwin's world, after all, survival of the fittest. But in the grandest scheme of all, I do believe that the push to win is threatening— even already eroding—this generation's happiness. Its happiness and its originality. Its capacity simply to imagine.

"Mom." I hear my name from the only one who will ever say it. *Mom.* I look up and see Jeremy, king of the hill, ensconced on a bench beyond the winged euonymus trees, beyond the canopy that was still green despite the ravages of summer. He is sitting there laughing, I can hear him laughing, at the promise that was not made but is kept. "Deer Berry," he is saying as I climb the steep and stony steps and reach him. "Windberry Holly. Lemon Balm. I read the signs."

Interference

SIXTH GRADE. A year in which tidy lockers and immaculately filed papers and neat handwriting rule supreme, while all that is intuitive, artful, and fantastic in Jeremy seems suddenly superfluous, misbegotten. His beautiful complex sentences are dismantled by a teacher who prefers just one noun and one verb between periods. His technically correct science papers are marked low for pencil smudges. He puts his math work in a green folder when the color of the week is yellow, he neglects to jot down his homework in the obligatory assignment book, his artwork falters under the weight of crooked lines, and many of his fifth-grade friends have morphed, over the summer, into cool and increasingly cliquish adolescents. What was inconsequential in fifth grade is not immaterial in sixth, and we're not ready for the bang of repercussions.

Jeremy suffers. Anxiety creeps in. He is relieved beyond measure on Friday afternoons and panic-stricken on Sunday nights, when Mondays loom. We should think about homeschooling, he tells me. I wish I could skip this whole year, he says. I wish I could skip being an adolescent. I wish I could go to sleep tonight and wake up tomorrow as an adult.

He stops showing us his papers, embarrassed by his misadventures with the rules. He stops volunteering anecdotes, and I worry. The guidance counselor is a godsend. She calls and talks about giving this time, about giving Jeremy room to find his way through this maze of superimposed stresses. She calls me, and I listen about transitions and about trust.

Trust your child. At the kitchen table I sit watching mine. At night I lie awake calculating the things I might have done—*should* have done—to prepare Jeremy for the rigor of this school year, this emphasis on form over content, this reality that those who don't accommodate and modulate will be asked to pay a price. The complex sentence will never persuade the teacher who exalts the simple, the green folder will not suffice when yellow's been ordained, the pencil smudge will offend on a desk where order reigns, and coolness is as coolness does in an evolving group of friends. These are the facts of life. At one point we must all take our stance toward codices and pressures. For Jeremy, that time is now.

I cannot know, at this juncture, how much of Jeremy's spirit will be subsumed by the coming year. I cannot gauge how his anxieties will mess with his dreams. I cannot guarantee that his gigantic imagination will get him through, to the other side of sixth grade. What I can do is give him tactics for survival. Tips on penmanship. Oversight on all transactions pertinent to folder hues and assignment books. Lessons learned from the cliques I skirted when I was a girl his age. What I can do as well is reaffirm my faith in his essential, creative spirit, let him know that there's always room in this house for the carnival of colors and characters that troop through, behind his eyes, for the fabulous if sometimes circuitous complex sentences that he writes. What I can do is stop whenever he says, Hey, Mom. I have this idea for a story. Hey, Mom. Let's read the new *Harry Potter*. Hey, Mom. Do you want to go to the arboretum? Hey, Mom. What would happen if? I can stop and I can listen while he writes and reads and dreams. To the tactics and the conviction, I bring the counselor's sage advice: Give Jeremy room to find his way. Don't ask too many questions. Don't fight his battles for him. Do not burden him with the worries that multiply in the petrie dish of this mother's mind. Mostly don't assume that his struggles are unique. This is growing up. This is where we are: sixth grade.

So I help where I can, and I pull back where I must, and I am there whenever Jeremy chooses to come to me with news from the frontiers of his life. The days go by, the weeks, the Friday sighs of relief, the Sunday tremors of melancholy, and then one after-noon, as we sit outside not doing much of anything after school, Jeremy lets me in on a plan. "I am going," he tells me, "to change the school. I'm going to make it a place I want to be."

"Tell me," I say, "what you are thinking." It's a quiet request, and I have to hope that he won't read it as a demand.

"What I'm thinking is that I'll organize a day where the fifth- and sixth-graders get to be the best at what they're best at," he says. "Everyone getting to be the best at something for a day. A sort of Spirit Day—you know, those wear-your-pajamas-to-school Spirit Days—only better."

I turn and look at him, really look at him. The tournament is an idea he'd had earlier last spring, when he ran for Student Council and won on a platform of "Great Ideas." But it was only a vague notion then, not fully developed, not philosophical in its leaning, and I had thought it had dissipated. Apparently, however, he has been scheming all this time, and I wait for whatever more he has to tell me.

"I'm writing a letter to the teachers," he says.

"Which teachers?"

"The fifth- and sixth-grade teachers."

"And what are you saying in the letter you're writing?"

"I'm telling them about my idea. Asking them for their support. You want to see the letter?"

"You already wrote the letter?"

"Um hmm."

"Well then: Of course, I want to see."

From his cluttered, clotted, never organized notebook, Jeremy pulls a sheet of crumpled paper. It's one of the three-hole-punch variety, though the punches have been torn through in typical idea-over-neatness haste. The handwriting is smudgy, hurried, not easy on the eye, so I ask Jeremy if he'll do the honors. "Dear Fifth- and Sixth-Grade Teachers," he begins and then continues:

I am writing this letter to ask for your opinion about my Student Council idea. I've suggested a sports tournament for fifth and sixth grade. This is not a Spirit Day, but this is a way to have fun without dressing up in costumes and pajamas and something that involves sports. Girls like Spirit Days a lot, but everyone loves sports. By playing sports, fifth- and sixth-graders will get to know each other better and have fun while they are doing it.

The dates that I've suggested for the one-hour sports tournament are November 21, 2001, the day before Thanksgiving break, and March 22, 2002, the day before spring break. The sports will be soccer in the soccer field, basketball on the blacktop, and kick ball in the baseball field. If it's raining, we can move all sports inside. People can sign up for being a player of any sport they want, being a referee, a fan, a cheerleader, a journalist, or even a national anthem singer. Each tournament takes an hour, and I would like to suggest that it be held from 11 a.m. to noon. The teachers could be either coaches or fans.

I hope you will agree that this is a good idea. Please let me know what you think about this idea.

Sincerely,

"So," I say, after he looks up from the letter, "the idea is to use team sports to help strengthen friendships and community?"

"Exactly." He nods. "Sports is a great way to make friends if you're not playing just to win."

"And the people who don't really like to play sports . . . ?"

"Can sing the national anthem if they like to sing, or cheerlead if they like cheerleading, or hang out with their friends in the stands, or write about it for the school newspaper, or commentate," he says, all in one breath. "We'll need a lot of commentators. And if they're really good with rules they can act as refs. And someone's going to have to talk about it on the morning announcements."

"Something for everyone," I say.

"Exactly."

"I'd vote yes for this if I had a vote," I tell him.

"Yeah. Because you're my mom. But what do you think the teachers will say?"

"Well, they might have some questions about scheduling," I tell him, wishing I didn't have to damage the dream with yet one more harsh injection of reality. "Or about safety or organization. I mean, it *is* a rather ambitious plan."

"Yeah. I know. But it's a really good plan, and it would make the school a great school, and I'm going to give out the letters anyway."

"Absolutely."

"And I'm going to see what they say."

"Sounds fair."

"Can you type it for me?"

"The letter? Of course."

"Oh. And I'll need lots of copies."

. . .

IT BECOMES A production. The typing of the letter. The Xeroxing of copies. The remembering of all the teachers' names. There is a last-minute decision to attach an addendum to each letter that fleshes out Jeremy's microdetails: *Every sport will have a referee. . . . If it gets really interesting sports commentators and national anthem singers might have to get dressed up. . . . If I need help with things like sign-up sheets and equipment, I will ask other Student Council members for help. . . .*

Through it all, Bill and I try to balance the dream with the reality, try to prepare Jeremy for the myriad roadblocks he'll in all likelihood encounter. We suggest—as gently as we know how to suggest—that the unassailable grandness of the idea itself might be finally insufficient to overcome established school priorities and schedules. We suggest that it might be awfully hard to persuade so many teachers all at once to give up academics for not just one sports day, but two. "I just want the teachers to *think* about it," Jeremy says, after we talk a while, and then the next day he says the same thing.

It's not that Jeremy doesn't get the magnitude, the complicated legitimacy of the many stated impediments. It's that he believes, in his words, that nothing changes anywhere until somebody stands up and hopes. He's hoping, he tells me. That's what this is about, and soon I come to appreciate that, no matter what pans out or does not pan out in regard to the proposed tournament, Jeremy is doing what he must do to feel more at home in sixth grade. He is envisioning the school the way he'd like school to be. Shaking off the paralysis of anxiety by putting this suggestion forward. "You can't depend on your eyes when your imagination is out of focus," Mark Twain once opined, and this is precisely what Jeremy is doing— sharpening his imagination so that he can survive what he sees.

This willingness to use his imagination to brave the crush of new rules and pressures begins, by November, to surface in the classrooms. The more attention Jeremy is forced to pay to smudges and punctuation and file folders and assignment books, the more he asserts his right to the original or the fabulous in his approach to the assignments. He converts a group writing exercise into an original rap song that he then performs, with two other boys, in front of the classroom—a wild success, I am led to understand by the teacher who graciously tells me about it later. He makes a deliberate choice about those complex sentences, choosing to write his own way and to face, *knowingly* face, the possibility of consequences. He draws the things he wants to draw in art, but does it more steadily, with a somewhat less crooked line.

By the time Jeremy learns that his proposed tournament will not happen—too much red tape, too many scheduling dilemmas, too many organizational quandaries—he has the wherewithal to take the news in stride, to push ahead to other things. He draws up plans for a proposed schoolwide talent show. He gets to school early to help the seventh- and eighth-graders decorate for their holiday dance. He entertains the kids in the hallways with the rap songs that he writes between his classes.

And then one wintry afternoon while we sit at the messy kitchen table, Jeremy casually mentions, amidst a host of other things, that he'd sung a song over the public-address system that morning and that most people seemed to like it.

"You did what?" I say, rolling the conversation back a little, then waiting for him to fill me in while he laboriously finishes his apple.

"The morning announcements, Mom. The canned-food drive. You know."

"Actually, no," I say. "What canned-food drive? And what song? And this morning, you sang? To the whole school?"

"Yup. It was fun."

"Did somebody ask you?"

"I volunteered."

"And what was the song you sang again?"

"The one I made up."

"What song did you make up?"

"Yesterday. In homeroom. When I was bored."

"How does it go?" I ask.

"I'll sing it for you," he says. I sit back in my chair and from memory he begins—his lyrics on top of the "Rudolph" tune, his pleasure compensating for his utter and helpless atonality. "Rudolph the can donater," he starts,

> *Was a very kind young man.*
> *And if you ever saw him,*
> *He would have at least one can.*

> *All of the other classmates*
> *Said that he was too worried*
> *Because he would bring all of the*
> *Cans that you would ever need.*

> *Then one shiny Christmas eve,*
> *His teacher came to say,*
> *Rudolph, your cans are all in sight*
> *Have a pizza party night.*

> *Then all his classmates loved him,*
> *As they peeled off all the cheese.*
> *Rudolph the can donater,*
> *You have brought in cans of peace.*

"You sang that to the whole school?" I say, somewhere between bemused and, well, bemused.

"Um hmm. Over the PA."

"That's pretty bold," I say.

"I know," he says. "But somebody had to get the food drive going because nobody was bringing in their cans."

. . .

I AM NOT TRYING to blithely suggest, when I tell these stories, that the imagination will rescue Jeremy from every last thing that comes along. I'm not trying to pretend that we're not still hitting pockets of terrible difficulties in sixth grade—kids who don't get Jeremy's songs, teachers who decry his messy notebooks, assignments that he complicates with a sometimes idiosyncratic perspective. I'm not trying to pull anybody's bluff; I know that competition—for the highest math scores, for the lead in the orchestra or play, for the chance to be distinguished as *extraordinary*—is seething all around us and that we will pay a price— *Jeremy* will pay a price—for not racing headlong into the fray. I know how many compromises Jeremy will still have to make to be the kid he'll have to be just to survive his adolescence, to get the grades and teacherly support required by anyone stepping forward, toward dreams. I live and work in the same world he does. I've been gently flogged and not so gently flogged for failing to conform to established standards. I have been rudely misunderstood, regardless of my intentions, and I know how it feels, as I have said, to stand in the margins.

But I also know—I firmly believe—that the imagination has been indispensable in a year during which so much is so suddenly at stake. The imagination, for how it helps one forge a bridge. The imagination, for how it buoys dreams. The imagination, for how it sometimes reels us in but also, at times, gives us sweet distance. The imagination, for how it helps my son define for himself just who it is that he is growing up to be. "Originality does not consist in saying what no one has ever said before," James Stephen once wrote, "but in saying exactly what you think yourself." This year, sixth grade, Jeremy is doing just that.

Paying Attention to Process

I WAS EIGHT GOING on nine when my parents took me to a frozen forest pond and helped me strap on a pair of skates. It was the hour before dusk—still enough sun to see not just the reflective surface of the rutted ice but all the rot trapped deep beneath—the tubercles of trees, broken twigs, last summer's dragonflies. I tossed off my hat and flew, catching the wind in my ears and the chill on my face and imagining all those dragonflies extending stiffened wings.

Life would never be the same. I'd go on to coaches and sequins and scribes, to Mohawks and spirals and speed, to footwork, to training before dawn. I'd delay my Axel, tuck a flip inside my splits, toe in for the double Lutz and spin: once, twice. The music fell, and I fell with it. It banged and chattered, pulsed and sighed, and so, of course, did I.

I grew up knowing that you quick-step your way through a pizzicato; that you deepen your edge to massed violins; that when the bass laments, you lament with the bass; that you open your arms wide to a plainchant. A held note is a spread eagle. A sudden polyphony is a combination jump. And when they play "Somewhere" from *West Side Story*, you are Maria—yearning, weightless, prayerful, subdued—and when they play a little Bolero you do as Torvill and Dean so bravely did: bend your knees to gather speed.

I carried what I learned from skating into the books I read. Melody, rhythm, tone, color, harmony, form: Such is music, and such is what I looked for in my books. I found it at the age of sixteen, in F. Scott Fitzgerald's *The Great Gatsby*, a symphonic book, an urgent book—so many instruments and interludes, so much raucous, furious speed toward the end. I found it in James Agee's *A Death in a Family*, which plays like a bow against a string and left me physically quavering. William Faulkner was choral as was the early Louise Erdrich, and when I discovered Michael Ondaatje's books I knew I'd finally found a skater. Ondaatje writes the way Kurt Browning skates—hypnotically, with a technical sophistication that yields up his soul.

And when I was writing, I was writing with the sound of oboes and violins in my head. Words are sound and color, both. They can be shaped into chords and rhythm, lesson, hush. They can be choreographed. It feels, to me, like skating when I'm writing. The blank page like the lull before the needle drops on the phonograph. The sequencing of chapters like the linking of flips and toe loops, footwork, lunges, the supining layback spin. The final edit like my final competition dress—beaded, delicate, refined at last, a banishment of excess.

We come upon our habits of mind in our own ways, with our own childhoods whispered into our present. Right or wrong, my work is haunted by my memories of ice. Fair or not, I cannot fall within the thrall of another's book unless it resonates with song. I am old enough to know that it's too late to change my ways. Old enough to recognize that I'll always be a skater.

Because still I wake in the hours before dawn. The skater's proclivity. After all these years, I still love—I still require—the essential qualities of darkness, the chill upon my face. Downstairs, I stand before the large old windows and peer out across the yard, dodging my own reflection. When I convince myself that I'm as ready as I'll ever be, I slip into my office and sling myself across the pinstriped love seat and read what I wrote the day before, scratching most of it into oblivion. I'll add a line or two, snap the piece apart, circle back, connect two fragments, hunt down minor chords and melodies. By 7 A.M, I'm out of words. I turn some music on—Schubert, Loreena McKennitt, *Man of La Mancha,* fandangos, Nelly Furtado, Bach, Norah Jones—it doesn't matter. What matters is that I can play it loud, that I can dance to it, that it rattles through my bones and loosens up my thoughts. What matters is how far the music takes me, and who I am when I return.

Afterwards, after I have stood inside the crush of music, I kiss Bill good-bye and drive Jeremy to school, then return to my reverberating house. Sometimes I turn the music back on. Most of the time I've got all I need inside my head—a bass, a plea, the tickle of piano, an oboe's desperation. I go back to the fragments, rush them together, snatch them apart, break things, make things, bury my face inside my hands. I stand and pace and press myself against the tall divided windows, whose fissures I'm aware of now that the sun has lit the sky. It seems as though nothing is happening, but almost everything is: I am skating, I am writing, I am lingering with story.

I will work until the music fades, which happens sometime near noon. I'll realize that I've been worrying the same sentence for an hour or more, or that I've lost the thread of my so-called idea, or that the verbs have lost their spunk, or that the adjectives are a distraction. Writers will say that their heads hurt when they are stuck, but it's my body that aches when my writing goes bad—

my body that feels the absence of music. And when my body aches like that, I grab my shoes. I go outside for a walk.

The houses in this neighborhood are (mostly) not pretentious. When we moved in nearly ten years ago, I had a feeling—irrepressible—that this pacific place on the west end of a train line would take care of that part of me that cannot survive without the infusion of music. There are, after all, these gentle hills. There are the soft corners on the streets and the old flowering trees in the yards and a patchwork of personal gardens. A few blocks over is my church with its red door, and it is right here, at this church, that the earth begins to give way, that the hills grow more steep, and the body is called upon to compensate, to shift its weight from heel to toe so that it might be carried down and down. I have walked this loop nearly every day since I moved in. I have walked it alone, a left turn, a right turn, a left turn, a long swooping arc, then up, up, up the hill, and right and left and left and home. The deer that live in the trees are not shy. They lope along like dogs on the asphalt or form a tawny concatenation—nose to tail to nose to tail—on the streets. I have seen red foxes along this stretch, and lovesick squirrels scrambling out of nests of leaves, and there is a bird feeder on one property that attracts a gang of goldfinches. In spring the cherry trees lay down their carpets of pink. In winter the nonmigrating birds stamp their talons into the snow.

It's not until I get to the church that I feel myself coming back to me. It's not until my body is forced to gather speed, and my ears are tuned to the songs of birds, and my eyes catch the shadow of a doe that the knot in my head starts to unwind. I don't try to force my thoughts. I don't try to fix the problem I wasn't solving. I merely breathe the weather in and out, and hope that something happens. Something almost always does. I am restored to music.

There are others in my neighborhood who walk, but I don't know their names. I know what time of day I'll see them, and I know the routes they take, and I know the look of concentration on their faces, the sound of their distracted hellos. That's all. I tend to think of them as being in the same profession that I am, the thought profession, I might call it, though I don't have a clue as to what they do.

JEREMY, AS IT turns out, has inherited this need to find an embracement for his thinking. In the beginning, I wasn't precisely sure what he was doing. I'd see him flipping his pencil or pacing the halls or walking around and around, and I'd worry. I'd listen to teachers complaining that he stares out windows before he writes, that he doesn't use his time "to best advantage." I'd sit with him and I would say, "Jeremy, maybe you should be doing *something,*" and he'd look at me and say, "Mom, can't you see that I am?" "But what are you doing?" I'd stare at him, frustrated. "I'm doing what I do, Mom. Thinking."

I'm thinking is, of course, an unimpeachable phrase. You can't look at someone and claim he is not. You can't get access to interior selves, internal triggers, mechanisms. You can't know when an idea is surfacing simply by watching the play of skin on a child's brow; an idea, after all, is not a tidal wave. And you can't always be accurate when you sling around that monstrous phrase (that I have used myself), *You are wasting time.* My mother says she knew my brother was thoughtful from the start by the way he studied carpet patterns when he was just a toddler. "But what was he *doing?*" I've always asked her, when she's told that story. "Looking at the patterns," she'll say, "and thinking. And so I left him to it."

Jeremy spends a lot of time just moving through space, and thinking. He is not, he says, listening for music; rather, he is watching the movies in his mind, or scheming up some riotous characters. I know no one else who has mastered the art of pure thinking with as much proficiency as Jeremy. He'll optimize the modest length of our hallways and dilate the apparent sizes of the rooms by slipping his body—practically incorporeal—between furniture and books. He likes to flip a pencil while he's imagining, and when he goes outside to be entertained by his own thoughts, he keeps a soccer ball at his feet—darts in and out of unseen obstacles, beats a weary path through the grass. He can even think while keeping the soccer ball airborne—by tapping it gracefully from foot to foot to upwards of eighty juggles. I have tried to juggle in this manner several times myself. Gone outside, stood beside Jeremy, taken my instructions. The ball bounces to the ground before I've been able to tap it from one foot to the other. I try again. I try again. And all the while, Jeremy is juggling, painlessly juggling. His ball never touches the ground. "Come on, Mom," he says. "It's not that hard." But it is, at least for me.

Jeremy writes after motion. That is his established sequence. As inexorable as the moon replacing the sun each night. As fixed as the numbers on the clock. "I'm going to work on my story," he'll tell me, and then he'll hurry outside and smash the grass blades to the ground, or skip upstairs and nub down the carpet. I am cognizant, always, of how it is in other houses, of how time is apportioned into measurable wedges. I think piano, flute, and violin. I think about the Japanese lessons he could be taking; about the Boy Scouts projects he could be doing; about the after-school club he could be attending; I even think about the books on his shelves that he hasn't managed to make the time to read. What is love, and what is intrusion, when a child is imagining?

Parenting is fractionally commonsensical. All the rest is improvisation and soul. I have had, throughout my journey with Jeremy, an idea of what childhood ideally is, and what I hope he will remember looking back. Friendship is essential in childhood. So are running and kicking and tumbling. So are music and art and drama and gardens. So is doing nothing. Teach a son how to cook. Teach a daughter to hammer. Take your child out in the crowds, but remember to also give him time to sit alone on the branch of a tree.

But between all one does to construe some semblance of balance for one's child, there is the need to shift the curriculum around who the child is. The need to allow the child to define himself, to listen to what he says. Jeremy tells me, when he is pacing, that he is seeing scenes, or making a plan for his next story, or on the verge—the very verge—of an idea. If I get close, he hunches his shoulders. If I ask a question, he hastily responds. If I say, "Hey, do you want to make the cookie dough?" he'll say, "Not now, Mom. I'm busy." He isn't being rude, nor is he being antisocial. He is learning about how he thinks and how he transfers that to paper. "Our boy has an artistic temperament," my husband will say. Just like his mother and father.

I have taught myself to trust my son's creative process by paying closer attention to my own. When he tells me he has an idea and then runs outside to juggle, I think how it is that music comes to me when I'm out in the neighborhood, accelerating. When he's flipping the pencil in his left hand while scribbling furiously away with his right, I think about the dancing I do, early every morning. To write this very paragraph, I first lost myself inside Norah Jones, and then I took a shower, and then I poured a glass of water, and then I sat in this chair at this desk before this computer and stared out the window at new snow. A neighbor peering in would be excused for concluding that I've been wasting time. But what I really think now is that I'm sticking with a process that I began to discover years ago, above the frozen wings of dragonflies. I'm yielding to my habits of mind, even as my son explores his own.

Surprise Endings

*J*EREMY IS ON the hunt for a surprise ending. He trails up and down the hallway, sighs, goes outside, paces the yard. It is October, the leaves have lately rained down from the trees, and as I watch him through the window I feel the melancholy of the season, the melancholy of a boy whose own story cruelly eludes him.

I can do little to help; I've already tried. We have sat with the sprawl of his long first draft between us, charting the story's terrain, hypothesizing plot. We have analyzed characters, settings, coincidences, motivations, the gaps between so many telling details; we have sketched out *what ifs?* with words and symbols. For weeks he has worried his mystery along with a seriousness that has become its own brand of worry, with a singleness of artistic mind that has made me wonder what I was thinking when I first seduced him toward writing.

At what price, writing? Outside, in the Chardonnay light of late fall, my son kicks at the leaves as he paces and grimly paces, while at this window I stand and consider all I've failed to warn him about stories and their making. What kind of love is that, I ask myself—leading my only child into the lair of writing without equipping him for its demoralizing hazards? Language is stingy, I should have said. Plots don't always yield. You can learn the rules of framing, form, and voice, but rules do not make stories. And you can love your characters as you love your friends, but that doesn't mean that they'll return the kindness, and you can deny yourself the noise of life, but silence does not leach language. Stories are inside us but they are also just beyond us, so that whatever you write, no matter how rare or good or true, will be subject to the scars of so much searching.

Jeremy wants, he says, to shock his readers with his ending. He wants a Harry Potter–style aha in a book that festers with devious adults, white-collar crime. He'll use conspiracy theories and lurking twin brothers and multiple locales, if he has to. But he won't be satisfied unless he hears, in his mind's ear, the collective gasp of his someday readers.

I want to surprise them. This has been Jeremy's refrain for the past month, at least, and the more he's dissected his own complex mystery looking for leverage and clues, the less willing he has been to call himself a writer. "The dialogue doesn't sound like people talking," he'll say of his own work. "I'm better at creating characters than I am at creating scenes." "The plot is not as interesting as it used to be, at least to me." Across the love seat in my office he has thrown himself like a fragile analysand, reading his story aloud to me so that I can type it and print it and read it back to him with new suggestive intonations.

I know what he is feeling. I know how desperate-making writing is, how it marches one out to the edge of one's capacity, which is never big, deep, wide, or, frankly, generous enough. I know what it is to be denied: not to hear the plaint in a character's voice,

not to feel the wind on the opposite side of the wall, not to see the
history in a garden plot, not to anticipate the future. Not to write
well, or to write too well, obscuring the larger purpose, which is
story. We are only as good as our own imaginations; the question
becomes, How do we take our dreaming further? How do we
improve on who we are and how we think so that the stories we
conjure up will somehow please us? We want to write exhilarating
stories. We want to surprise ourselves.

Reading other people's work is a partial cure, but this Jeremy
already knows, has taken deeply to heart. Above his bed is that
shelf of books, and on that shelf are the ones he loves—*The
Phantom Tollbooth, The Call of the Wild*, the Lemony Snickets,
the Harry Potters, the Roald Dahls. And in those books are his
own fat circles around sentences that thrilled him, characters he
rooted for, plot twists that surprised him, strokes of genius. My
son understands that story rises out of story, that we stand on
shoulders and stretch up. He understands that to be a writer one
must, first and always, acknowledge those who write for us.

But beyond reading and practicing and playing his thoughts off
the page, how will he find what he is looking for? Even after all
this time, after all these years, after all these private conversations,
I am not in complete command of any one answer. I struggle to
know what to do for my son, who is outside disturbing the leaves
like the antihero Charlie Brown, while inside his mystery tarries—
on note cards, on torn scraps, under his bed, beside the canister of
flour, on my computer. He doesn't want to be suggested to. He
doesn't want to borrow. He will not compromise. He is the only
one alive who can write his story's ending, who can finally pronounce who stole the race car and why and how severe the consequences will be.

"Mom," Jeremy said to me, before he went outside, "I hope I
don't always want to write; it is too painful, it is just too hard."
Closing the door before I could find an answer; leaving me here,

at the window, watching him. Because, yes, writing is almost always too hard; it can feel like a curse, a condemnation. It can feel like a room without windows or doors, or like a tree without its leaves, exposed to weather. It can feel like nothing, endless nothing, a stoppered life, a broken dream. Yes, writing is almost always too hard, except for those breathtaking times when it isn't—except for those almost ineluctable moments of deliverance when the lair's lamps burn bright and the air carries a scent and through the silence one hears the chitterings of language. Writing is almost always too hard, I will say to Jeremy, later tonight, except when the story blows in.

A Few Like-Minded Souls

ALMOST ALL THE stars have departed from the ceiling of Jeremy's room. You close the closet door, shut down the lights, look up, and you might see a few discs of neon yellow-green, but nothing that suggests much more than a constellation's fringe. The closet is more like a filing cabinet now, with its reams and reams of paper, its soccer statistics and comic strips, its unfinished stories, character lists, puzzles, spur-of-the-moment slogans, and hand-drawn magazines all providing evidence of a mind at work, not to mention a most determined keeper. Throw nothing away: That is Jeremy's mantra. I might want to look at these things tomorrow, he says, or remember them when I'm grown up, or I might need to consult them for another project. Throw nothing away, and in addition to his closet, there is his room—his desk, his shelves, his drawers, his floor, the space beneath his bed—all piled high with the pulp of former trees, and one floor away is the kitchen table, half of it given over to Jeremy. How Jeremy knows where anything is is beyond my understanding. Why he won't see the logic in my own tidiness and order is a matter that we seem to talk around, without making any headway.

Don't disturb the paper in Jeremy's room, and don't disturb the plastic minions, the universe of Lego and Playmobil figures that Jeremy rules like a benign dictator. These little stiff-legged figures with the Botox smiles are all actors in Jeremy's Saturday-morning television hours, afternoon movies, commercials. For the past few weeks there's been a corner of Jeremy's room all done up in *Who Wants to Be a Millionaire*. There's a Playmobil Regis Philbin and a Playmobil audience and a rotating cast of Playmobil contestants. The questions asked are the ones Jeremy makes up—consulting encyclopedias, history texts, the Internet, workbooks, his own indubitable sense of humor until he's generated what seems to him a fair selection. When the curtain rises on the show, Jeremy is puppeteer, musician, emcee, Regis, every contestant, and every member of the audience.

"For two thouuuuusaaand dollahs," Jeremy-cum-Regis is saying, "What is another name for a stoop that you sit on? A, a step. B, a block. C, a dumb person. Or D, a roof. Take your time. Use a life line, if you need to. Remember: This is the two-thousand-dollah question."

Silence now, and then the music, all these little bleeps emitted from Jeremy's lips. When Jeremy (now the contestant) gives a weak squeak of a response, Regis takes over again: "C?" Jeremy raises his voice, ups the ante on the accent. "Did I hear you say C? A dumb person? Well, congratulations, Marty, because C . . . issssssss . . . correct!"

Wild audience cheers and whistles, a catcall from behind Jeremy's hand.

"Now," Regis says, to the weak squeaking contestant, "for four thouuuuuuuuuussssssssand dollahs, answer this: What kind of dog plays football? A, a German shepherd. B, a golden receiver. C, a Great Dane. Or D, a poodle."

"A golden *receiver*?" I say.

Jeremy gives me a look. "It's the joke version of the *Millionaire* show, Mom."

"They have a joke version?" I'm ribbing him, and he knows it, but he plays along.

"Not on the real TV, Mom."

"You're making this up?"

"I'm allowed," he says, and then he returns to the show.

It's a beautiful thing, watching Jeremy's imagination at play, a funny thing too, more and more, but I find myself conjecturing, as I slouch in this beanbag chair, what might be happening at this very moment if Jeremy had been blessed with a brother or a sister, a single best friend—somebody his age or almost his age who would know intuitively how to maneuver these Playmobil characters, how to enter this stage, how to go right foot to the left foot of Jeremy's diverting tango. It isn't about spending time so much as it is about sharing a specific turn of mind, and if friendship is equally serendipity and soul, if it is not the place of parents, after children reach a particular age, to intervene, I nonetheless concern myself with the question of companionship. When Jeremy's friends from school stop by, they mostly play soccer—a good thing, a great thing even, but not, in Jeremy's case, quite enough. When the book club ends for the summer, it ends *until* next summer; there are too many pressures on most of the kids' schedules to conduct the program through the academic year.

Jeremy assures me that he isn't lonely, that he looks forward to these hours in the afternoon when homework is done and the house is quiet and he can do whatever occurs to him, for whatever reasons. I grant him that. I need my aloneness, too. But I do think it would be better if he had a few like-minded friends, kids with whom he might share the dreams in his head, the books that he reads, the thoughts he is translating into language. Friends with whom he might feel *validated,* beyond the womb of family.

Last year, for a little while, we had that here, when a family of six temporarily moved in next door while they awaited the renovation of a new home. The kids were half-Irish with a wholly Irish mother, and they had this marvelous endowment of zeal, so that when the three boys were here, there was fanfare and clamor, grand outtakes of laughter, a perpetual trail of cookie crumbs, and when the daughter came, she and I stayed downstairs, talking books. She'd borrow and read, she'd come back and we'd discuss, while above our heads the sound of boys would pound against the walls, ricochet through the hall, vibrate down the steps. We had the family for dinner. They invited us into their home. The boys did Claymation together and joked together, they played games like Mancala and Riven. And then we shared a Christmas Eve and all of them were gone.

"Jeremy," I say, pushing up now from this chair. "I'm going to make a call."

DOWNSTAIRS I GRAB my address book and hunt for the number of my friend named Karen, a mother of four but also a writer of prodigious talents who published her first novel to wild acclaim just a year or so out of college, but rather than rush back into the world with a second headliner, Karen chose to become a mother. Lauren first, then Madeline, Caeli, and Pascale, who is better known as Calla. Karen chose to become a mother and to listen, as her girls grew up, for the aspirations and affinities that would soon define her daughters. Lauren, as it turns out, has become the daughter of ideas; she reads and thinks, articulates, defines, suggests, proposes, and asserts. Madeline, for her part, likes to sing and to perform; Caeli has mastered the violin; and Calla draws the most amazing things—careful Magic-Markered patterns that glisten in the sun.

"Karen," I ask, on the phone, when I reach her. "Why don't you bring your daughters here?" For Jeremy, in fact, has never met them and I've only seen them once or twice myself. They live forty-five minutes away, and they are perpetually busy, and Lauren, the eldest, cannot come. But after Karen says yes for the rest of them, we set the date, we say good-bye, and I go upstairs to relay the news.

I find Jeremy on his bed, his eyes turned up, toward the ceiling, his face alive with pleasure. "What are you doing?" I ask, standing in his doorway, my weight against the frame.

"I'm imagining something."

"Yeah?"

"In my mind."

"I see." Except, in fact, I do not see; his room is silent. There is only the flicker of the sun. Only the noise of the street, which is vague and episodic. Only Jeremy, lying on his bed, watching the Technicolor in his mind, not turning to see me, not flinching. "Is it a memory?" I ask.

"No. It's a story I'm making up."

"A good one?"

"A good one."

"At the start or almost done?"

"Just starting."

I have been on the phone; I want to tell him Karen's girls will be here in a few days. There's homework waiting downstairs; I should do the parental thing and get Jeremy going. But here I stand at the threshold of Jeremy's private cinema, watching his face while he watches his thoughts, watching the sun shift, watching and waiting for some odd, impossible suburban calamity to waft up from the street. I stand here and he lies there with his inviolable imagination. Inviolable, impenetrable, both fleeting and defining. "Tell me about it later," I say. Or tell the girls, I think, when they get here.

A FEW DAYS later, I buy an overly ambitious tropical plant—yellow and red stripes on oversized Crayola leaves—that requires an entire corner unto itself but accentuates the colors of this early autumn. I buy what we will need to eat, and then fifteen minutes before Karen and her girls are due to arrive, I ransack every closet looking for a decent tablecloth. I go with the wrinkled one without the stains; it's like serving lunch at sea.

Am I doing the right thing? Do I have any business thinking I can suggest my son toward new friendships? I feel embarrassed, all of a sudden, sitting at this oceanic table with Jeremy, Karen, and her three daughters—embarrassed by the stultifying politeness I seem to have induced by asking too many preliminary questions of one almost twelve-, one nine-, and one seven-year-old girl, each of whom is pretty in an entirely original way and seems inclined to check with her mother first before scooping out more tuna, or talking. Alchemy isn't in a parent's hands, I am reminded. Only circumstance. You can bring as much party as you want to a table, but you can't make it sing.

And so I stop. I just stop talking and sit back and let the kids take over, make room for Caeli, indeed, to ask a question of Jeremy, who tells her something about his school and then lengthens the story, because she nods; she lets him gauge her interest. She's all blue eyes and haloing hair. She's an ember of a child, but then there's something precociously composed about her too, something anyone would respond to, and Jeremy does; Jeremy returns her questions with his own, so that now Calla, the artist with the exquisite cheekbones, has something to say, and Madeline is laughing, shaking her head of dark hair.

There is the fragile bloom, in this room, of chatter. There is

Caeli turning the wheel of the conversation around to her fascination with Japanese and Calla talking about Shakespeare and
Jeremy, who doesn't know much about either thing, saying,
Really. Really? in different voices. He does an English accent and
a southern one, eliciting another encouraging giggle from
Madeline, and then Jeremy says, leaning in toward the girls, "Do
you want to see my room?," leaving Karen and me at the table
with dessert, where we talk about books, our own dreams. Every
once and a while we hear fragments from the *Millionaire* show
above—a chorus this time, and not a solo—and later there's the
sound of Chinese checkers, someone teaching, someone learning,
the advance of marbles under way. I am more grateful than
Karen, a mother of four, can imagine for the afternoon she's
brought to us—for the noise in my house, for the spirit of friendship, for the clemency of children's games.

AFTERWARDS WE HEAD off for the thirty-one-acre pleasure
garden just down the road from my house. It's a place that I discovered last spring, a place I most often go to be alone, to prepare
for the blaze of incoming weather or to sit in a swarm of butterflies. At this garden, it is landscape as stage sets. Flowers as character, a foreign language, a Chinese lantern, a swatch of velvet, a
purple star, a bowl of cotton. It's hydrangea, string beans, false
sunflowers, the crowning pink of water lilies and the nesting of
wrens and the emergence of apples on espaliers and the creeping
of roses between the beams of pergola. When I go to this garden I
look for the frog that neither fears nor fits inside my hand. I watch
the thorough collapse of things, in the aftermath of exuberant
blooming. I rarely take anyone but Jeremy to this garden. Today I
have the urge to share it.

We're barely through the front gate when the kids are flying—
down the hill, where the daffodils cascade in spring, across the

thin finger of the stream, toward the pond, over to where the once-tall ferns are a flattened molten brown. The kids run past the lilies—staunch and burnished, long shorn of pink—and the singed cornstalks and the reds that have yielded to yellows, and the trees, with their emigrated leaves. Corms and rhizomes, fibrous roots, rosettes, stems, and simple leafs, the gourds that have grown overheavy for their vines—the kids run past it, through it, by it, intent on a game they have agreed to.

It's not a big place, but Karen and I have lost three girls and a single tall boy for the moment. We wend around on the asphalt path, following the superimposed order of the garden while somewhere just beyond us are the kids. We are aware of their laughter erupting from beneath the huge skirts of trees. We hear their echoes reverberating off the potting shed. We catch sight of one or another of them sprinting, cowering, climbing; this is a game of hide-and-seek with a dash of something auxiliary that I can't read from where I am with Karen. This is the way it's supposed to be. Kids being kids, with other kids, the imagination shared, not stowed.

The Little Critic

T HAS BECOME the winter of movies, a tradition that's crept up on us and somehow bound us to it. It is suddenly on Jeremy's top-five list of things to do, and he has taken charge of our Sunday afternoons, poring over the entertainment magazines, reading reviews, studying the marquis of the theaters we drive by. Whatever is rated PG-13 is fair game. Action/adventure is preferred. Popcorn is a prerequisite; he likes his without the butter. I tag along desperate for the occasional art film, the relationship film, a little romance. I tag along and give him lots of harmless grief.

"But something's got to *happen* in a movie," Jeremy protests, when I yearn for the old days of *Hannah and Her Sisters*, when I shake my judgmental head at Jackie Chan.

"Friendship *is* a happening," I say. "*Love* is. Come on."

"No. I mean *happen*, Mom. I mean really *really* happen."

"You owe me," I tell Jeremy, while Bill pays for the tickets and I buy our popcorn. We head into the dark and find our chairs. We're the only ones, at least right now, in this neighborhood theater.

"You can rent your kind of movies when I'm at school," Jeremy tells me, through a mouthful of popcorn, a slurp of soda.

"And watch them alone? Are you kidding?"

"Why not?"

"Well, for one thing: Whom would I review them with?"

"I guess that's right."

"And for another: I like my popcorn popped at the theater."

So we go to the movies on Sunday afternoons and we sit as a family and take our entertainment—Bill, Jeremy, and I, and whoever else drags themselves in. Bill *gets* these movies that Jeremy loves. He's as wide-eyed as his son, as willing to suspend his disbelief, root the good guys on, be entertained. Unless they've yielded to a movie like *A Beautiful Mind* or *I Am Sam*, I am happier watching the two men in my life watch their movies than staring at the silver screen itself. Side by side, all lit up with fiery flicker, Bill can look like a kid again, and Jeremy can look like the future.

WHEN IT COMES to Sunday afternoons, I look most forward to the critiquing afterwards, when we're back at home, munching the last of the leftover popcorn, rotating the afternoon's feature in our minds. As the self-anointed movie aficionado, Jeremy has rigged up all these evaluation *methods*; he's got his categories and subcategories, his extra considerations and politics, a numerical ranking system that is no mere thumbs up, thumbs down, thumbs sideways.

"What are those categories again?" I'll ask him while we all sit around the table, and he'll rattle them off: Scenes, Story, Characters, Setting, Ideas, and Subject. Every category is graded independently, 1 through 100. Then the numbers are tallied and divided, and the result is Jeremy's score. The difference between a 92 and a 93 is never accidental, I assure you, and when a movie doesn't live up to its advance billing, Jeremy looks for ways not to be critically offensive. He'll pad the "Ideas" category of the film that's short on scenes, and if the story line is as riddled as a slice of Swiss cheese, he'll give the movie extra credit for its subject.

"You are nicer," I tell him, "than most critics I know."

"Really?" he seems interested. "How so?"

"Well look at this," I say, picking up one of his movie scorecards from the end of the kitchen table, where they reside unless we have a guest for dinner. "You gave *Star Wars: Attack of the Clones* a 94, but the acting was just terrible, and the story was only so-so."

"But, Mom—you're forgetting about the setting. You're forgetting that part of it took place in that place we went to in Seville."

"You mean the pavilion in the Parque de Maria Luisa?"

"Yeah. That one."

"And that's enough to keep the ranking above 90?"

"Well, think about it, Mom. How many sci-fi future movies have you ever seen where you've actually been to one of the places where it was filmed?"

"None," I say. "You are absolutely right."

"So it gets a 94, and I'm keeping it at 94. It fits."

"But you gave *A Beautiful Mind* a 92."

"Of course."

"But it was *such* a wonderful movie."

"It was. Except where it was slow."

"Slow?"

"Yeah. When Russell Crowe was just sitting and staring."

"What? You mean toward the end? When he's taking all those meds?"

"Yeah. That part. I'm sorry, Mom, but that was just a little dull."

"I don't think we are going to agree on this."

"Well, these are my opinions."

"Fair enough."

"And you want to know what else?"

"What's that, Jeremy?"

"Dad agrees with me."

I look at Jeremy, then Bill laughs out loud. My kid gives me one of his sly, appealing looks. "This is when I start to think that you should have had a sister," I say.

"You can have your own opinions, Mom."

"You're right. I guess I can. And given that, I'd have to say, I would have given *Clones* a 70."

"Well, I like to be nice to most movies."

"Why's that?" I say, while to myself I think, Where's Jeremy when I need a good book critic?

"Because I *like* movies, to begin with," he answers. "And because, did you ever think how hard it would be to make a perfect one?"

IT'S A GOOD thing—a great and also endearing thing—that the impossibility of perfection does not keep Jeremy from trying. Does not keep him, now, from this newest sheaf of papers upon which he has begun to write his own screenplays. I don't even know what he's doing at first; sometimes I do lose track of all his projects. But when I see page after page being written in red, I take notice and ask questions.

"What are you doing over there?" I ask. It's a cold day, gray and flat.

"Script," he mutters.

"A *movie* script?"

"Well, it's not for a play." Jeremy does not lift his head up. He's writing at furious speed, and his fingers are bloodred with the ink.

"What's it called?"

"'*The Salesman Who Wins a Half a Million Dollars.*' Inspired by *Rat Race*. You know."

"What's it about?"

"About five salesmen who work for a place called Shop City who have to get from Baltimore to Milwaukee to win a prize."

"That does sound like *Rat Race*."

"Yeah. But all the jokes this time are about selling and sales, and there's lots of funny stuff with cars."

I lean over his shoulder, take a look. Sure enough, this is a movie script. Top of page one is THE BACKGROUND STORY. Middle of page 1 is CHARACTERS: SCENE 1. Bottom of page 1 is SCENE 1, and then there's dialogue, with lots of cueing about gestures, movement, sound tracks. "How did you know what a script looks like?" I ask, puzzled by the professionalism of the setup.

"Remember the play, 'Stone Soup'?" Jeremy says, trying to keep this short, I can tell, to brush me off, get back to work.

"I do."

"Scripts, Mom. I've seen them."

"Well," I say. "Well. Carry on."

A FEW DAYS later I am driving Jeremy to school when he announces, matter-of-factly, that he's finished his salesman script. "Done, as in completely done?" I ask.

"Yeah," he says, nonchalantly. "So this afternoon I'll start another."

"Okay," I say. "Sure." And then there's silence. I look at him, out of the corner of my eye, this child who will be my height in perhaps a month or two. His voice has started to change; I hear it pitching. There is the first soft down above his lip. Girls notice him when we're out together, and he's taking new care with his clothes. Sixth grade, with its stifling emphasis on organization and its narrow band of standards, with its growing cliquishness and stultifying social strictures, has not been a happy year for him.

He's been curing himself from the anxiety it has induced with his portfolio of projects.

"Mom?" he says, after a long moment in which I understand that he's been negotiating with himself, thinking about ways to be gentle.

"Yes?"

"You know how I always said before that I was writing just to be writing?"

"Yes."

"Well now, that's even more the way it is."

"What do you mean?" We have pulled up to a red light. I turn to look at him directly.

"Well, writing books, Mom, like you do? That's a pretty quiet life." He looks me in the eye, and I can tell that he's had this on his mind not just this morning, but for a while.

"I know."

"And it's fine for you, because you're a mom, for one thing, and for another: You don't even like action/adventure."

"That's mostly true."

"But I like action/adventure, and I want to live an adventurous life, and I think it would be much, much better to direct movies than to sit at home by myself working on stories. So I'm going to be working on scripts now, okay? And when I write stories, I'm going to think of them as movies. I'm not going to worry about writing the details, even though I know you like details. I'm not going to describe what the character looks like except for what he's wearing, because a character always looks like the actor. And when I want to explain who the character is, I will explain it with dialogue."

"I think that's great," I say, full of respect for all the things he's thought about, a little concerned about the particulars. "You going into movies, I mean. I think that's great." I thought, I think, that I'd made it clear: I've never wanted Jeremy to be a writer. I've wanted him to learn to write, to imagine out loud, to take solace from stories, to articulate what he thinks. "Nothing has really happened until it's been described," Virginia Woolf said; I've wanted him to *describe* things. I've wanted him to believe in the value of a dream, to explore, in his own heart and mind, the kinds of questions that stories make us think about. Morality. Consequences. Triumph and forgiveness. I've wanted him to know himself, not to work toward a profession.

"You're the bestest, Mom," Jeremy says, studying my face, looking relieved, scratching his cheek with his long finger. "You and Dad. The bestest. But also . . . ?" And now we're crossing the bridge and we're almost at school and he has to hurry up.

"Yes?"

"I'm going to be writing action/adventure movies, not relationship movies, because I am a guy, after all."

"If they're your movies, I'll be there. I promise," I say, turning into the school drive now, pulling up beside the door.

"Good," he says. "Okay. We're here." And he vanishes; he's gone.

AT HOME I go to Jeremy's piles of stuff and retrieve his script. I sit in the pale winter sun at the kitchen table, and read all thirty-two single-spaced pages, something I had promised him I'd do. I try to picture the scenes as Jeremy's written the scenes, and I am helped in this by the two-page casting list I find amidst all the paper. The slightly unstable store manager, Nigel Wick, will be played by Alec Baldwin. The maniacal police officer will be played by Robin Williams. Tim Allen, Kevin Bacon, Chris Rock, Seth Green, and Rowan Atkinson compose the sometimes bumbling, sometimes greedy cast of salesmen; Barry Bostwick will stand in as the Shop City owner; and for comic relief partway through the film, audiences will be treated to a musical number performed by

Cuba Gooding Jr., Martin Lawrence, and Wayne Brady, with Jason Alexander "nervously" directing.

It is action/adventure all right. It is Jeremy's brand of offbeat humor in collision with Jeremy's politeness. Most of these characters say "thank you" at least once over the course of the movie, while simultaneously dallying in the preposterous. One of the salesmen boards a bus with the rock band that sings in every city. Another drives a Ferrari across a farm. Still another optimistically hops into a passing race car, only to be slowed by the driver, who gets all caught up in the crowd that is roaring for autographs.

"Don't you know you are driving a race car?" the frustrated salesman asks the driver.

"It's a race car, not a racetrack," the driver says.

"And both a Ford Taurus and a Pontiac GrandAm have just passed you."

"And now I'm hungry. Let's eat at this Italian restaurant."

It's page after page of high jinks, gags, and slapstick, of emotions so close to the surface they pop, of some silliness that only a kid would understand and some allusions that only a movie fan might catch. Here again is an almost adolescent, but this one isn't looking back, this one isn't second-guessing; this one is in full control of his unexpected ending. The half-million dollars go to Jack Blower, brought to you by Kevin Bacon. The final words on the very last page are: *And the audience claps.*

I shuffle the pages back together, slip the casting list onto the pile's top. I sit in the kitchen surrounded by silence and consider the person my son is becoming—his own person. There is nothing here, in these pages, that I would have suggested to him, nothing that reflects his time with me, his lyric-minded mother. I hardly have a sense of humor; he is shot through with one. I hardly know how to get my own fictional characters talking; Jeremy's forte is dialogue. I rarely note what my characters are wearing; this script notes every stripe on every tie. It would be great—I think—if Jeremy would develop these characters further, greater still if he paid more attention to tension and buildup, even better (I myopically opine) if he wrote a part for a woman, for his is a two-page casting list that calls solely and exclusively for male actors. And maybe some of the technicalities are off, and maybe I don't get the part about the rubber horsehair, but what is my role, I sit here thinking, how can I help this beginning screenplay writer? How much *should* I? Where is the line between trespassing and guidance, interest and vested interest? What is a nudge? A shove? A fracture? How do we support and yet not trample? How will I keep my own worst impulses in check, and what will I do when I can't?

Sitting here I think of how, for these past many years, I have been, above all else, a mother. Vigilant and on guard, uncertain, unqualified, marginalized, and idiosyncratic, and yet endlessly hoping to do right by the child I have loved perhaps too fiercely, if one can love a child too fiercely; about this I remain undecided. Sitting here I know, as I have always known, that mothering is never just about the heart. It is equally about the mind. About the questions that can't be answered and yet hang. I have only one child, and every day is another day gone by. I do what I can, aware of all I should do better, of all the mothers out there, somewhere, who have a grander plan. I shuffle Jeremy's papers, and I stand. I pull the spices out for dinner.

A Community of Writers

HE KIDS COME to my house over eight weeks this summer. They come on Thursday nights before the sun goes down and play outside until it is too dark to see. Inside I light the family room with amber-emanating lamps and centrally locate the rocking chair and try to keep focused on the most important thing—to make not just words but being together a celebration. I spread a plastic tablecloth across the floor and release a five-foot-tall flamingo balloon that walks, as it turns out, on its own accord upon perfectly creased crepe-paper legs and cardboard feet. This flamingo will lose weight but it will never die; it will never stop roaming this room. It will walk over pretzel bowls, stand steadfast on clipboards, crane its long neck to steal a view out my windows. It will do what it wants unless it is swatted or laughed away, and in all of this it will have a helium companion, a three-foot-tall smiley-faced balloon that likewise peregrinates on paper feet.

We begin with T. S. Eliot, Robert Frost, Edgar Allan Poe, and the question: What makes a poem a poem? Rhyme and meter, metaphor and simile, stanzas and lyrics, the length of lines—all these things, the kids answer, talking over one another, raising their eyebrows, laughing. But fundamentally, I ask again, what must you have to make a poem? Much thinking, much laughing, and then the answer: Words. "Words," I say. "That's it. You need words to make a poem," and I ask for a list of favorite verbs and nouns, then for a list of synonyms and opposites. Then I ask the kids to name the two balloons, to put those names on their list.

Nine months have passed since *The Call of the Wild,* and in the intervening months these kids have grown taller, more fluent, more emotionally combustible and opinionated about almost everything they do. The girls sit with the girls on one side of the tablecloth, and the boys sit with the boys, and sometimes shy glances are exchanged as they pass the lemonade, and sometimes silly remarks. There are thoroughly untraceable outbursts of giggles. Plenty of puns. There is Jeremy among them, joking, doing his silly voices, surprising the others and me with his perpetually original contributions. Jeremy thrives in the hubbub of this club. I watch him bask in it.

By fiat and without argument the kids decide the flamingo shall keep its store-given name, which is Fletcher. After considerable communal debate the second balloon is made to answer to "the Godfather." "Come on, Fletcher, speak to me, speak to me," one of the girls, Gabrielle, keeps saying. "What do you want?" Daniel says to the Godfather. "What do you really *really* want?" "Oh look, they're dancing!" But throughout the distractions and the play, the poems get written, read aloud; I don't even have to urge. Verbs and nouns and synonyms kick, shimmy, strut, and some poems rhyme and some don't, and some are pointed and some are lyric, and every time a poet begins to read his or her work, another kid goes to fetch Fletcher to make it listen to the words.

"What do you learn from the poems you've written?" I ask, when everyone is finished performing. Looking back at their clipboards, the young poets think a little, then offer whatever comes to their minds. "That I stink at rhymes," one says. "You do not," another counters. "That it looks better when I break long sentences up into little bits of words," says one. "That metaphors are hard," says another. We talk about assonance and alliteration. We talk about the difference between storytellers and punners. We talk about who likes to ride the wave of the lyric and who likes to get snippy or jazzy, who feels safe getting personal and who likes to keep his or her distance. Then we choose our favorite bits from each of the works and use these to springboard us to the next exercise, and this in turn leads to something more, until we are out of lemonade. Another lightning bug makes its way inside, embellishing the ambient amber. The room is never perfectly quiet. Even after the kids go home this first Thursday night there is the clack and shuffle of cardboard feet, the sound of a lightning bug's wings against the ceiling.

I am interested in the kids being *interesting* this summer, in their learning to recognize and to tell interesting stories. I want them to feel free to take risks, to feel safe experimenting, to go out on that limb and take us with them. We work on beginnings, characters, and dialogue. We snatch lines from "Casey at the Bat" and "The Raven," from *Tom Sawyer* and *The Hobbit*, from Ernest Hemingway, Dorothy Parker, and Eudora Welty, and try to compute what makes them work. We gather headlines from various magazines—"Terror at Dusk," "The Art of Reflection," "Taking the Long View," "Pitch Perfect"—and consider possible plots. We work on first person and third person, telling the same story both ways, and we give ourselves few-word combinations—"bad hair day," for example, or "missing button"—and fashion entire characters around them. If the Godfather begins to retreat to one corner, if he gets a little saggy and deflated, Fletcher never loses his prying ways. Even when he detaches himself from one of his accordion legs, even when he gets so thin that Tiernan calls him anorexic, he is always there in the middle of things, tapping down beside the kids' clipboards, nosing his face over their shoulders, perpetuating the festive.

We look forward to Thursdays, Jeremy and I. We look forward to the cacophony in the house, the combustible energy of eleven- and twelve-year-olds, the books that get carried in and passed around, the commentary we don't see coming. We like being with the others as dusk yields to lightning bugs and lightning bugs cede to stars and the amber of the room intensifies. Sometimes some of the girls come early to help me set up or to talk about a story they stayed up all night to read, and I ask them for help with a book I'm reviewing. Here, let me read this to you, tell me what you think, does this opening scene make you want to read more? Sometimes the boys hang around after the writing is done to play soccer in the dark, and I hear Jeremy cracking jokes in foreign accents. In my mind, and in Jeremy's mind, it is about friendship first. It is about using language for what language is for—for conversation, for exploring, for discovering.

Our last night together we take everything we have—the phrases and fragments, the strategies and impulses—and build a neighborhood. Instead of a tablecloth, I roll out long sheets of glossed white paper, tape them together, sprinkle the room with colored markers. Instead of leaving Fletcher to limp across the floor, I fill the room with fresh balloons. I put out two kinds of juice, the necessary double bowls of popcorn. With two fans spinning, I turn the lights down low, ask each of the parents as they drop off their children to come back a little later than usual. Then I ask the kids to settle in, to take their places around the paper.

Using handouts I'd prepared a few days before, the kids focus on the development of a character. Just one character per boy or girl, each character fleshed out with a name, a nickname, a physical description, a wardrobe, a designated speech pattern, three child-hood memories, an indication as to job and hobbies, a list of three significant possessions, and four particularly salient features about his or her domicile. It's an exercise that produces, among others, a Britta, a Jean-Pierre Comodeschampe, an Emmy Jane Harris, a Fran L'Turnip, and a Solangus Sustarstic, the last of whom sports milky white hair and reddish violet eyes and has taken up residency in an asylum. Before the kids get to draw these characters on the paper spread before them, they draw and color up their homes, enthusiastically transcribing ideas into shapes and color. It's what you'd call a mixed neighborhood—there are a castle, a haunted house, a run-down joint, an upper-class builder's home, and several more traditional residences now sitting side by side.

Only after place has been established do the kids lodge their characters inside the grab-bag neighborhood. It is a frantic, fever-ish, funny undertaking, with colored pens being pitched around the room and balloons trailing colored ribbons across the work and laughter erupting all over the place, mostly the artists poking fun at themselves. But once we have place and people, we have the starting point for story. We have the questions: What would your character do if he or she got saddled with these neighbors? Who here, in this town, gets along? What does conversation sound like among these idiosyncratic constructions? How would Britta's inability to finish any sentence she begins rub up against Jean Pierre Comodeschampe's habit of turning every thought into a rap song? How would Emmy Jane's predilection for calling everybody "Suga" go down with Fran L'Turnip, whose cheeks are too pink, whose entire wardrobe is a bathrobe, and who cares most strangely and most deeply for Dungus, her dung beetle. "What's going to happen in this neighborhood?" I ask. "What tensions are going to erupt? Who will have the wherewithal to restore the peace? Who will sleep through it all?"

Choosing a neighbor to the right or left, the kids conjure up fantastic interplay. They develop drivers who are disrespectful of cyclists, women whopping men in bar Ping-Pong, characters contemplating themselves in mirrors before getting on with the day, rabble-rousers and complainers. Writing stories first from the perspective of their own characters and then from the perspective of characters others have created, the kids' primary job is to get inside the heads of these original people. To be empathetic. To try to understand what makes strangers do what they do and what the consequences are of fixed behaviors. "You can only manipulate a character so much," I counsel. "You have to be consistent. Try to make sure that everything that erupts or festers or is in the cards can be traced back to the original profiles."

I could not ask for better company. I could not have a more exquisite time than I am having, right here, in my old rocking chair, watching the kids, listening to them read, watching them listen to one another, stealing looks at my son, Jeremy, the rangy kid in the thick of it, a huge smile on his face, a satisfied smile: I am here, and I belong. No one could—or should—ask for anything more than the song that is playing in this room, the cool air that has blown in, in the heart of a long hot summer.

The night runs out on itself before the characters are finished speaking, before the conflicts are resolved, before the friendship that might have congealed between Fran and Solangus has a chance to solidify, which is the way, I have discovered, of these summer sessions. The postulated neighborhood is overwhelmingly strewn with intrigues, arguments, and affairs, lost jewelry, near apologies, escaped dung beetles, sentiment, and who, in any night of any life, could tie up so many brazen, fabulous, convoluted, fetching, delicious loose ends? Who would want to call it to an end? Who wouldn't ask for another hour?

But the parents have begun to show up on the stoop, and the stars have supplanted the lightning bugs, and school will begin in a few short weeks. Once again, our time is over. The kids stand, straighten themselves out, collect their clipboards, leave the paper on the floor. A few of the girls hug me good-bye; Mary hands me a jar of preserves. Stephen raises both hands for high fives; Daniel leaves me with a glorious yellow bowl. And then they all file down my narrow hallway and drive off in their respective parents' cars.

I am already projecting ahead to next year and hoping that they'll want to come back. I am thinking about how Stephen showed up at my house one hot afternoon to ask if I would mind if he wrote about a dream he'd had. How Daniel—the pianist, the actor, the kid with an undeniable gift for stories—gets everybody laughing each time he reads his work out loud. I am thinking about the creator of Fran L'Turnip, who writes with such enviable, grace-ful ease, and about her friend with the huge vocabulary and about all the books the kids pass around because they've read them and they want the others to. I am thinking that I am lucky that the par-ents go along with this—stop whatever they are doing and get in their cars and drive their children to a place where the sole reward is the time they spend in the company of the imagination.

Next year or the summer after that I will ask the parents why. Why do the kids come here? What are they looking for, and do they get it? And when I hear their answers, I will come to under-stand just how much these parents have also been seeking a sanc-tuary for their children's dreams. How they too have been wondering why the writing of kids is classified as right or wrong, as better than or less than, in classrooms across the country. Why there is so much emphasis placed on math and science, but far too little favor shown to reading, writing, and imagining. One dad will tell me he wants to poke a stick into the fire and stir things up. Another will ask when more college admissions folks will begin to celebrate the stuff that can't be quantified. Another will ask when childhood became such a bad or shameful thing, something to be hurried through, shaken off and forgotten. Who is going to change the world twenty years from now? these parents wonder. If winning continues to be so important so early on, what will happen to politics, or, conversely, to compassion? Why aren't there more forums for the *what if* questions.

I know the imagination can be as dangerous as it can be healthful. I know that books don't cure all things and that dreams can take us places that we really should not go. I know these things, and the parents of the workshop kids know them as well. All any of us is hoping for is a little more room for conversation, a little less stifling competition.

Prolific

A T THE KITCHEN table, I find Jeremy engulfed: by paper, stumpy pencils, a crumby eraser, tall stacks of research. It is late afternoon on a winter day, and his homework is done — rushed through so that he could get to projects. Everything he's written lately is within his reach, buried, maybe, but somewhere nearby on floor or table or sideboard. "Mr. Money's Lemonade Cans," a fantasy fashioned out of rhyming couplets. *The Secret of the Prime Minister*, a novella of jagged twists and turns. A colored-in floor plan and building section that exposes the interior of the fictional "British National Headquarters of TV Game Shows" and showcases the respective beehives of activity: the "practice" room, the game-show question development room, the sit-com advertising room, the celebrity dining hall. There is a character sketch of a New York City detective named Robert Nolan George; a list of the gadgets favored by spy Adam Rogenzapp; a document that underscores the personal secrets of assorted enemies of state; and a chart called "Mystery Characters Graph: Stories 1–7" that details the crimes, settings, nationalities, business ties, and role allocation of an evolving detective series. There are two handwritten and hand-colored soccer magazines, pages of Magic-Markered storyboards, lists of potential (always fictional) political candidates, and story synopses for Jeremy's own as-yet-unwritten screenplays:

BEAVIS AND BEACON
Comedy
Starring Cuba Gooding Jr., Wayne Brady, Morris Chestnut
Sony Pictures
Rated G
August 22

>   Beavis and Beacon (Gooding and Brady) are the owners of a Burger King who can't find a way to advertise their restaurant until they find a jazz musician (Chestnut).

POLITICAL CELEBRITIES
Comedy
Starring Robin Williams, Owen Wilson, Michael Caine
Warner Brothers
Rated PG
July 10

>   The head of a game-show network (Caine) cannot find good-enough game shows for his channel, so he asks two game-show hosts (Williams and Wilson) to run for mayor of Chicago so that he can televise their debates and speeches.

SPORTS IN THE SKY
Science Fiction/Comedy
Starring Charlie Sheen, Robert De Niro, Barry Bostwick
Columbia Tristar
Rated PG-13
July 11

In the year 3000, American sports leagues have decided that the athletes must play in the sky. An MLS Columbus Crew member (Sheen) does not know how to stand in the air, so the Crew coach (De Niro) and assistant coach (Bostwick) help him.

THE RIGHT ROCK STAR
Drama
Starring Mark-Paul Gosselaar, Ewan McGregor, Sylvester Stallone
Universal
Rated R
June 24

A music production executive (McGregor) will fire one of his music attorneys (Gosselaar) unless he hires the right rock star (who becomes Stallone) in less than a week.

"Mom," Jeremy finally says with a sigh, after some time has passed. "There's just so much work to do. Always. I'm never going to finish."

"Why would you want to finish?" I say. "It's the doing that's the fun part."

"Yeah," Jeremy says. "But it will be better when I'm grown-up. When I can actually make some of these movies."

"So you're still going to be a movie director?"

"Yeah. Or else a spy."

"You'd have to live your whole life in secret," I say. "If you decided to be a spy."

"I know. But just think of the gadgets."

He works; he never lifts his head. I slip across the hall into my office and sit down at my desk, sink my face into my hands, and turn on my computer. All the scraps of my thinking are lodged in a machine, and I envy Jeremy his vibrancy and sprawl, his endless options. All the people, places, possibilities in his head. All the flavor and fancy of an unfettered mind.

He is doing what he is doing because it gives him pleasure. He knows that soon I will sit with him and read through his work, and that sometime after dark, Bill will come home from the city, sit at the kitchen table, tell us something about his day over dinner, then push back his chair and take a look at the work his son has been "up to." What have you been up to? Bill will say, reading Jeremy's stories out loud. He will give silly accents to the main characters, profess excitement, surprise, interest, delight, then tell Jeremy his favorite parts. Jeremy is still working with an indulgent audience of two—his father and I. For now this seems to be enough. It gives him a reason to keep going.

I, FOR MY part, keep going too, keep figuring out these days, as one by one, with their own surprises, they come. I have learned, for one thing, to take a slightly more than passing interest in the James Bond movies Jeremy loves so that I can appreciate the myriad adulatory influences in Jeremy's myriad Bond-inspired projects.

I have learned, as well, the names and mechanisms of assorted spying equipment—the waist-belt surveillance camera, the through-the-wall viewing camera, the copy camera, the folding monocular, the fiberscope, the pen with microphone, the pen that unlocks, the pen that takes pictures, the pen that contains a map and compass. I have learned not to rush to judgment about whether an espionage mission is technically feasible; consider *GoldenEye*, I'll be told, or *Dr. No*. I'm allowed to ask about character motivation but told not to push too hard: "You can't always tell why someone in real life is being mean, can you? You can't always tell what's in their mind." I'm tolerated if I suggest that we've seen a few too many bright silk ties, but challenged as to which silk ties should go: "They're all great designs, Mom. You would like them if you saw them." I'm not appreciated when I speak of the appalling lack of women in Jeremy's screenplays; even if I have actual facts on my side—*consider Odette Sansom or Violette Szabo*, I might say, after checking a spy book—I'm rebuffed: "These are my movies, Mom. I get to decide."

But mostly what I seem to be getting best at is providing Jeremy with grown-up resources and then walking away. Jeremy consents to the knowledge found in books and on the Internet—the knowledge in almanacs, the knowledge in spy dictionaries, the knowledge on movie and CIA Web sites, the knowledge in books like *The Forensic Casebook: The Science of Crime Scene Investigation*. I'll find him upstairs curled up with *The Crime Writer's Reference Guide* or *Trial: The Inside Story*. I'll find him studying books like *How Come?: Planet Earth* and *The Big Book of Tell Me Why*.

Beyond the facts, of course, there's the question of craft, and Jeremy's hunger to write better comes not from me but from what he reads, from what he sees other authors doing that he can't quite do himself. When he, for example, reads Agatha Christie now (and he reads almost all of Agatha Christie's books), he's not just trying to unravel the clues before the solution is revealed; he's trying to figure out how Christie tells the story—how she positions the evidence, introduces the characters, gets readers interested. When he watches the movies based on the Christie books (arrived recently, in a box from my mother), he avidly studies the translation from page to screen, sometimes watching the movie twice. He can tell you what's idiosyncratic and what's expected, in a Christie book. He can tell you which story kept him guessing. He can tell you how what he's writing has been inspired by Christie, and how it deviates, and why.

He knows more about his genre now than I do. At the same time, he has the maturity of mind, the generosity, to sit with me and ask me questions about the work I try to do, to compare my literary objectives to his own, to listen to the stories I myself am struggling to write, to offer advice. "Jeremy?" I'll call to him, from my office, if I'm stuck.

"Yeah?"

"You have a minute?"

"What? What is it? What's the matter?" He'll appear in the doorway, tossing a pencil with one hand, his socks half off and floppy.

"Nothing's the matter," I'll tell him. "I just wanted to see you."

"It's the novel, isn't it," he'll say, entering the room and plopping down on the love seat, throwing his long legs over the armrest the way I'd once tried to teach him during the days of learning to read alone. Now the position suits him just fine, I could bring him a book and I could lose him to it, but I'd rather talk instead.

"Yes," I'll say. "It's the novel. It's my main character, Luis."

"I knew it." He'll toss his pencil into a double somersault. He'll never move his eyes to follow its acrobatics, but his hand will reach out and blindly catch it.

"I'm stuck," I'll say. "It's pretty bad. I can't make Luis come alive."

"Well that's because Luis is dying, Mom. You shouldn't start a novel like that."

"But he has to die, Jeremy, that's the story," I'll say, though Jeremy knows what the story is, for I have read him its early chapters. "It's a story about the end of a life."

"In my opinion it is much, much better when something happy happens. You should give Luis something to do besides dying. In my opinion, you should make him a spy." The pencil goes up, flips, nods to gravity, falls into his palm.

"In your opinion . . ."

"Or at the very least, a detective."

"But I don't write detective stories. You do."

"Well, you should try, because I think that being a detective is more interesting than dying."

"I don't even know how to write detective stories, Jeremy. That's your specialty."

"Mom," Jeremy will say, "it isn't that hard. You watch Agatha Christie movies and then you watch James Bond, and you come up with something in the middle."

"That sounds hard."

"It's a lot easier than writing about dying, Mom. Or at least it is in my opinion."

What, I think, I would give for the autocracy of Jeremy's mind. He has the capacity, as most children—given time—still do, to make the leap into the unfamiliar, the unprecedented, the unknown. He has the wherewithal to entertain the ideas that show up in his head; he's not afraid of them. The imaginative mind must feel free to suggest the spirit of a thing without falling captive to its form. It must be willing to climb without ropes, to jump without out a net, to yield to the unknown. Jeremy knows where his imagination *is*. He knows where to find it. He launches a pencil into somersaults and trusts his hand to catch it blindly.

On Becoming a
Compassionate Writer

HE BEES HAVE come inside my house this summer and stayed, as if they could find water here or relief from the endless sun. They have huddled together against the window glass, a living hive, and not even Springsteen's *The Rising* has displaced them, not even the slow drawl of *To Kill a Mockingbird*, which I have been reading out loud to Jeremy on the couch beneath their huddle. The bees have come to live with us, and they endure, as we do, the heat, the blinding stifle of dust outside, the premature exhaustion of the trees beyond the glass.

It has become the summer of disbelief, also despair. It has become the summer of missing children and forest fires, of pretty girls with bombs on their backs, of a few men's greed and a market's sloppy tumble, of terrifying talk. It has become the summer of the timid seeking rescue and the brave holding their tongues and marriages under private siege and so many kids away at sleepover camp that Jeremy and I are fundamentally on our own. I go in for the classics: Harper Lee, John Steinbeck, William Faulkner, Eudora Welty, Flannery O'Connor. We read near the bees and we read in the arboretum and sometimes we drive in the other direction, toward the garden, where we sit beneath the canopy of a tree or beside the diminished gurgle of a stream. I read the books as much for me as I read them for my son. I read them for the pleasure of floating the sentences in the air, for the intelligence of Jeremy's commentary, for the distraction from the news, for the pleasure I know he's getting as each day, early and unprompted, he says, "When are we going to read the story?" Together we try to make sense of those two same hats in "Everything That Rises Must Converge." We attempt to figure out what justice means in *Of Mice and Men*. We read *Mockingbird* more deliberately than we read the other books and talk about conviction. If there is any teaching going on, then both of us are students.

In the mornings Jeremy decides, again, to pick up his writer's pen; he's got a screenplay in his head, he says, but for now he feels like "regular" writing. Poetry, journalism, contemporary fiction, historical fiction, whatever he or I manage to come up with: He's game, he asks for this. I give him exercises that I have done myself or exercises that I find tucked inside books like *The Writer's Block*. Here's a good one, I'll say, and then I'll read from *Block*: *"Tell the story of a job interview that goes badly. The more your character wants the job, the better the story will be."* "You can put as many silk ties as you want to in that tale," I'll kid him, and he sits at the table and works.

It's when I suggest that he write some personal essays that his genuine enthusiasm dims. "I don't like the idea," he says, matter-of-factly, "of writing about myself. I'm just not comfortable with it."

"The *idea* of it?" I say, a little thrown.

"It doesn't seem very interesting, Mom. I mean, I already know about myself, for one thing. It's more exciting to imagine what I don't know."

"I can see your point," I say, "except that I do think we have to imagine if we want to know ourselves. We have to remember, for one thing, and we've talked about how remembering is like imagining. Then we have to look at ourselves as others might see us, and there's a whole lot of imagining in that. And also we have to imagine what it all means—what we mean, what the world we live in means, why the things we do might or might not matter."

"I'm not convinced. I'd rather write fiction. It doesn't seem fun, personal writing."

"To be honest," I say, after a moment, after I've thought about it long enough to be certain Jeremy's ripe for the conversation, "I've had questions about personal writing myself."

"You have?"

"Yes, I have. Always. But it's not the exciting or fun part that worries me. It's lots of other stuff."

"Like what?"

"Like the risks I feel I've sometimes taken. Writing about myself, and others."

"What do you mean?"

I look at him—this adolescent with the grown-up's face, this companion in the land of literature—and tell him what I've tried to think through, solve. I tell him the things that I have learned to consider when I sit down to write from life. The importance of finding the universal in the personal. The importance of the word *resonate*. The importance of teaching oneself how to write out of heart toward heart, out of hurt toward healing, out of memory toward hope, which is all different, I say, than writing to exploit or to expose. I tell him I try to keep some verbs in mind when I write from life: *Explore* as opposed to *trump*. *Suggest* instead of *prove*. *Protest*, not *pronounce*. *Propose*, not *demand*. *Discuss*, not *win*. *Record*, not *brag*. I tell him that I think it all comes down to motivation in the end, to compassion, and that sometimes I know I fail at this, sometimes I worry that I've betrayed, sometimes I regret the exposure, but I keep trying. I feel *impelled* to do it better.

"Do you think I'm a compassionate writer, Mom?" Jeremy asks me now.

"I think that's your impulse," I say. "But it all takes time and practice, and you can't get better at it if you don't try. Why don't you try to write something personal. Just see what comes out. For the heck, as you say."

If he's not entirely enthusiastic, he does concede to trying. Here I want to be perfectly clear, to say again something that I have said already in the pages of this book: I am not pressing Jeremy to write memoir because I am hoping that he'll be a memoirist (Lord knows, the world has plenty). I am encouraging Jeremy to think about himself, to reflect on who he is, to find his own language of self. Self-knowledge is my purpose here. Wisdom. We can talk about these things until we are blue in the face, but we cannot impose them upon our children. We can simply ask them questions and hope that they'll want to respond. Talking about self is one thing. Writing about self gets us further.

To get Jeremy started, I buy him a copy of "The Autobiography Box: A Step-by-Step Kit for Examining the Life Worth Living." The packaging of this product so intrigues him, the *sophistication* of it, the fact that it's really intended for adults, that he studies the instructions eagerly and flips the workbook open on his own. I let him be. A few hours later he tells me that he's answered all the questions he cares to answer, and hands me the workbook and heads outside.

I turn the pages. I slowly read his responses to the queries. YOUR RELIGION an early page is titled, then: "What church or temple did you go to as a child? What part did religion play in your life?" *I go to church,* begins Jeremy's reply. *But religion doesn't affect me that much. I agree with the idea that all things are created through God, that God helps people, and to be kind to others. I disagree with the idea that God is with us and that we have to love our enemies.*

YOUR STRENGTHS headlines another page: "Can you pull a tractor with your teeth? Can you keep your checkbook balanced? Can you cook dinner and watch three kids and talk on the phone all at the same time? Write these strengths down." *My strengths,* Jeremy has written, *include creativity, great long-term memory, I am easy to please, I am kind to others, I tell funny jokes, I am very close to my parents, I find good things to do with my time, I don't watch TV until 8 P.M., I am good at soccer, my grades are As and Bs, and I am adventurous. I can do impressions of many fictional characters, and when I sense something is going to happen, nine out of ten times I am right.*

YOUR WEAKNESSES the next page begins: "Do you always buy impulse items at the checkout counter in the store? Does a pretty girl's smile elicit special treatment? Have you wasted whole days watching television?" *I am overly sensitive to insults,* Jeremy confesses. *I can be obsessive in some ways and messy in others. Whenever I am bored I express that feeling. I don't read directions as carefully as I should.*

All of this is true, I think as I read, but also only half true. A boy coming to terms with himself.

THE NEXT DAY, Jeremy rises early and comes downstairs and lays out his writing tools—lead pencils to flip, lead pencils to write with, colored pencils to help keep ideas in order. It is time, he says, to start working on his series, and so he begins by sitting and staring. Then going outside. Then coming back in. Then staring.

But the wheels in his head are making a racket—I can see it in his eyes—and this morning will be the first of many mornings of moving forward with what is in his mind: *The Lieutenant Lapper Mystery Series.* An elaborate, illustrated eight-part serial that is written in story form but meant (in Jeremy's words) to be *experi-enced* like a movie. The Lapper series places its eponymous hero on the case of stolen nuclear missiles, the assassination of ambas-sadors, the backroom dealings of double agents, the murder of a passenger on *Air Force One*, and the raiding of American military equipment. It will run to more than one hundred single-spaced handwritten pages by the time it's done, be bound inside a hand-drawn cover, offer up a table of contents, and, to entice Jeremy's audience of two, come equipped with its own back-cover blurb:

> The Lt. Lapper series is similar to the Hercule Poirot series in that it is a mystery series and it has similar clues like murder disguised as suicide. But this series is more like James Bond solving a mystery. The crimes are politically-motivated. With the exception of a newscaster, a journalist, a professor, a car-penter, and a priest, all of the suspects work for some govern-ment agency. In fact, each mystery has 5 or 6 suspects. There are gadgets like a watch with a flashlight. Two of these myster-ies have traps and two have nuclear technology. But what is most like 007 is Lapper, D. R. Lapper. He is not a detective; he is a spy undercover in the Air Force. Unlike Hercule Poirot, Lt. Lapper is very serious and since he has a "license to kill" he often shoots who he convicts. This series has eight mysteries.

In a summer of poetry, journalism, contemporary fiction, his-torical fiction, and essays, in a season of insufferable heat and widespread gloom, Jeremy is finally settled in with this, his hand-chosen metier. He is turning the story form into the *feeling* of film, and he is teaching himself how to do it. He is reading *Double Indemnity*. He is studying books about 007 and watching a John Grisham rerun and heading off to the mystery writers' section in the bookstores. Sometimes, at his request, I'll read him Stephen

King's *On Writing,* censoring out the not-for-adolescents parts and focusing on the tips. Sometimes I'll read to him from an old copy of Agatha Christie's *An Autobiography,* wading through the filler on debutante dances and early nursing years until we hit some mother lode. When we get to the part in which Christie finally explains how she conceived of Poirot, her famed Belgian detective (the inspiration coming, as it turns out, from the number of Belgian war refugees in England at the time), Jeremy looks exultant.

"So that's it," he says, sitting bolt upright on his bed. "That's why Christie made her detective Belgian. And made him tidy. And made him talk about his gray cells."

"Every character comes from somewhere," I say.

"Yeah," he says. "But I'd been wondering how she came up with such a finicky guy. I couldn't figure it out. You know my Lt. Lapper? The one from my series? He's a mix between Poirot and Bond."

"So I've seen."

"He's got a lot of funny traits. I hope my readers like him."

BY SUMMER'S END, Jeremy's series is as implacable as the bees. He'll stay up late to write and get up early to illustrate. He'll flip his pencil, pace the halls, go outside to do that thing he does with the soccer ball. He'll give me the dailies to read—three or four handwritten pages—and I'll admire and prod and sometimes, unfortunately, get too involved, too *critical.*

"I'd love to see more of that landscape or that view from that window," I'll say. Or, "How about a few lines about the guy's childhood?" or "I think I know more about this detective's wardrobe than I do about his feelings." When I press too much, Jeremy gives me that *you promised* look, holds up his hand, and mentions Stephen King.

"Didn't Stephen King say something about writing to your strengths?" he'll ask, a rhetorical question.

"Something like that. I guess."

"Well that's what I'm doing, Mom. I'm writing what I'm best at. Writing to my strengths. My strengths are plot and mystery."

"But you can work at all the rest," I say, 100 percent certain that I won't win this battle today. "Character and nuance. Details. Foreshadowing. All the good stuff."

"Every story gets better, Mom. You've said so yourself."

"That's right."

"And I'm having fun. Isn't that what you want?"

"It's what I want."

"So can I get back to my story now?"

"Yes you can. Absolutely."

THE LAST WEEK of August is hotter than all the days that have come before. It is thoroughly insufferable, and the bees know it and I know it, but Jeremy, so much his own person now, is unaffected—so at home in his own imagination, so invested in this series. *Read it like a movie.* I circle near but mostly do my best at giving him some distance, so that now we work in separate corners of this house, measuring the world with words, unraveling certain skeins of yarn and making something of the wool. When Jeremy finishes another section of his series, he brings it to me. When I finish a scrap of something, he lets me read it to him. He sits on the beaten love seat in my office, his head thrown back, his eyes half closed, his lips perfectly still as he listens. I'll know when something works just by watching his face. I'll know what's broken by the crinkle in his brow. I'll know how sacred these moments are and how, soon, they will drop away from us, like the stars from the ceiling.

For Jeremy has turned thirteen this summer. He will be shaving soon. His voice is different. He is talking about getting a job, likes to go into town on his own, sometimes sees movies without us. There are "ladies" he alludes to, but he won't tell us their names. He does such a mean James Bond impression that he is known, outside the family, as 007, and what he knows and what he believes have become his own possessions. What he does with his talent is of his own choosing. He is original, his own kind of person, and just as it has been my job to help him define himself, it is my job now to let him *be* himself, to give him the room that he needs. To love as much as I have always loved, but not to hold him in love's vise. I must get myself ready for middle age, I think. I must face the inevitability of absences and distance. I must imagine myself toward the future.

On His Own

ILL AND I sit at the local café with a crème brûlée and cookie. We are older, twenty years older, than the crowd, and shy with each other, the way we get when Jeremy's gone. *Don't go far in the woods, Don't fly off the trampoline, Don't watch the movie if it's gruesome,* I did not say to Jeremy when I dropped him off for an evening with his friends. Could not say, because he's grown-up now: a tower of a boy halfway through thirteen.

The love in this room is young love. There are barbed-wire tattoos where wedding bands might be, silver rods plunged through the skin, a tease behind so many pairs of eyes. If Bill and I are too old for this, no one says a thing. If we wear gold instead of ink for rings, we are allowed our loving too.

We take our romance where we find it, Bill and I. The theater of our love affair has been our bed, our stories. Stolen kisses, rented movies, the weather on our roof at night. We never dated.

Not in cafés. Not over desserts. Not in a roomful of strangers. Not in the pause before a song. Tonight, out here, it's awkward, odd. Tonight we feel our age among young lovers.

My husband is a man made more beautiful by time. The years have turned his black hair white but they have not etched his face, and the folds in the lids above his eyes have softened his expression. The ring on his finger is loose because his hands are tapered, slender, and I have always loved his faded jeans, the twisted leather on his wrist, the size of him, his slenderness. Any woman would notice Bill; they always do. Even the ones here, in this room tonight, would love a man this decent. If they knew what kind of father he is, they would love him even more. If they knew how his hands feel against the skin, they wouldn't let him go.

We almost dated once, when we first met. Almost dated, but we never really did. We just came to know each other. We just came to fall in love. He came to love me, but he would never tell me why, never say more than "Just because." But I was never at a loss for the words that suited Bill. I had adjectives and poetry, the testimony of the heart. All Bill had to do was draw, and I was mired. All he had to do was walk into the room or play the guitar or touch my hand, and I'd lose my sense of reason. We're skipping over the dating part, I used to tell my friends, though in truth, I didn't know how to date this man; I knew only how to love him.

So here we are in a café, middle-aged among new love, our son somewhere out there in the dark of this night, flying off a trampoline, I'm sure, and watching a B movie. The hands in this room are touching other hands or they are cradling warm coffee or they are holding up pierced faces, waiting, and what I'm thinking of, as I also sit here waiting, are my friends and all their sorrow. Their stories about the end of love. Their stories of implosion. Marriages are collapsing, marriages as long as my own. Marriages and love affairs and homes that I once sat in. I have done nothing but listen. I have done nothing but urge courage, caution, kindness, the only advice that I can offer. I have imagined my friends. I have imagined their lives.

The crowd at this café tonight cannot know what twenty years will do to love. They cannot know how romance wears, then reasserts itself, then shifts inside the music. The girl beside Bill teasing the boy beside me. The two at that table, making like tonight is forever. Here is love, in this café, and here am I, on a shy and also tender date with the man who is my husband, our son in the world on his own. I don't know how I look to him, or even why he loves me. I don't know what questions I might ask, because he's told me all his stories. I don't know how to be beautiful, how to urge him closer. Come closer, Bill, I almost say. Come closer now, and kiss me.

We are waiting for the music, for the songs of three young men, playing a bass, a guitar, and a keyboard, which, now, all of a sudden, appear. The musicians stake out the back of the room; they settle behind mikes, before the hush. They sit and adjust and test out the sound, they measure the crowd, they begin. They play music they have written in a basement or a garage. They play music that's in code, the script of love. Who doesn't want to surrender to the young men tonight? Who doesn't want to be here, in the genesis of song? Who doesn't want to watch as the musicians press their hearts against their notes, as they close their eyes and sing?

I am watching Bill as he watches them, as he picks up their rhythm with one finger. I am watching my husband as he concedes and yields and softens to the riddle, as he thinks—it's in his eyes—about our son. "Bill," I say, "Bill?" and he takes my hand, and leans and slowly kisses me, and we leave and drive home now, together. The house is quiet and dark. We hear the sound of our footsteps in the hall. We slip through the shadows of the night, for our boy is out in the world.

No More than That, No Less

HOUGH IT IS late fall, I am spring-cleaning, relieving the house of broken things. Discarding the fractured glassware, changing the color of the ceiling, tossing the fissured fireplace tile, replacing the ruined kitchen floor, redressing the woodwork, the doors, the upstairs hallway, jettisoning all those things, so many things, that are not worth keeping. This is my project. I choose the colors—peach, cream, bright white. I stand on the stepladder and spackle. I free the kitchen cabinets of the inhospitable goblets, sweep glistening shards into the dustpan, put a suite of new goblets into place. That which I cannot fix I cover with fabric. Those things that I cannot afford appear—miraculously—as gifts. Across the tops of tables, mantels, radiators I sprinkle the gold, copper, and green skeletons of dipped ficus leaves, and then I announce that I'm throwing two parties—a dinner, near Christmas, for Karen's family of six and a later buffet for friends.

In the midst of all this, Jeremy's busy. I'll find him in the basement at Bill's computer, researching something for a project. I'll find him at the kitchen table, hovering over his spy files, working out the names, occupations, aliases, success and failure rates of his imaginary spy missions. Sometimes, when he runs outside to see a friend or to kick the ball around, I'll discover a page he's left behind, some floating detached ephemera that's been fashioned quickly, set aside. The synopsis of a screenplay he's got in mind. A list of character names and funky occupations, for future integration into plotlines. A statistical accounting of themes already explored or trick endings previously exhausted. A poem about his middle name, dashed off in pencil, on a torn sheet of notebook paper:

NAME POEM

William is in the middle
But not many know it's there.
It is like a spy,
Undercover in myself.
Only friends and family know him.
Only family even speak of him.
He has no alias.
He just is hidden inside my name.
Not even on my ID
Not anywhere but here.

And yesterday I found Jeremy upstairs on his bed, reading a biography of Steven Spielberg. Just curled up in the position that he's now decided works best for him, the library book pressed flat against the quilt. "What are you doing?" I asked him, and he said, "Studying Spielberg."

"What are you learning?"

"That he was a kid a lot like me."

"Yeah?"

"Yeah. He grew up in the suburbs and he liked imagining things and he was always making movies, he always knew he wanted to."

"And look at him now."

"Still making movies." A sigh, long and meaningful. "I wish I'd known him. That would have been cool."

"People will be saying the same thing about you, in a few years."

"Maybe."

"But I'm glad I know you now."

"Me too."

"And I'm looking forward to your movies."

"So am I."

He turned on his bed, rearranged the book, and curled more protectively around it, a sign for me to head downstairs, which I did. And I didn't return to his room until later in the afternoon, when, intent on painting the battered woodwork in his room, I find something hurried into existence, left behind:

STEVEN SPIELBERG POEM

If I had known you well
I would have probably been your friend.
We would have had so much in common.
You would have been interested in entertainment
Just like me.
I would have shown you my stories
That are meant for movie screens.
We would compare your films to my stories.
You would tell me tips for creating films,
Spy and mystery films in particular,
And I would give your movies great reviews.

Now, the Friday before Christmas, Karen's family has promised to come. The Humpty Dumpty house has been put back together, and I have spent the morning at the market, the afternoon in the kitchen with turkey, white wine, black olives, tomatoes, capers; with chunks of tuna and pasta and handfuls of parsley; with spinach, pears, pecans, a vinaigrette. I've bought the kids three games that span their ages, and Jeremy's job is to clean his room so that there'll be sufficient space in which to play them. I have the music up loud, the candles in their votives, the Christmas tree alive with lights when, hearing the phone ring, I put down my whisk, turn off the song, and say hello.

"Beth? It's Karen. How are you?"

"I'm good. I'm happy. How are you?"

"We're good and we're almost ready to go, but Calla and Caeli wanted me to call and ask if they can bring their instruments tonight. If they can play something they've been practicing for Jeremy."

"Of course. You didn't need to ask."

"I told Caeli it would be fine, but she thought I should call and ask you first. She said it's rude to just barge in with a violin."

"Tell Caeli her music is always welcome here," I say, laughing. "Tell her I'm getting dressed for the performance."

And I do. I change out of what I'm wearing and find a long black velvet dress, put something sparkling in my hair, something glittery on my eyelids. I tell Jeremy, too, that we're in for some live music, and he decides on his own to dress for the part, to welcome this minstrelsy in his way. By the time Karen and Larry and the four girls get here, we are ready for anything—for the meal, the conversation, the laughter that tumbles down from upstairs where four of the kids have gone to play "Imaginiff." Beside me at the table, Bill catches my eye and I catch his, and he doesn't need to say a word, because I know what he is thinking, I feel the way he feels: that Jeremy is precisely where Jeremy belongs—in the company of companionable souls who imagine out loud, as he does.

The music comes later, much later, when the wine is gone and the table is cleared and we feel the exertion of the icy black air against the window glass. Beside the Christmas tree, Caeli stands and plays, while the rest of us sit, a serrated horseshoe. Two movements of unaccompanied Bach; a piece by Fritz Kreisler called "Syncopation." Caeli's a tiny thing with a gigantic presence. Her giganticism is her joy. Her face catches the light of the Christmas tree as her hand frisks the bow across the strings and a few strands of hair escape her ponytail. The room fills with sound, as if the stereo is on. The notes arrive in astonishing clusters; I can't imagine how Caeli does this. If Karen knows all the notes of this piece, if Larry, Lauren, Madeline, and Calla do too, they watch Caeli perform as if they've never seen her play before, as if she is teaching them this song for the first time.

Caeli wants to play, has chosen to play. There is no boast in this performance, nothing to prove but a child's pleasure. When Calla stands and joins her and they play "Pat-a-Pan" together, the circle of song grows that much stronger. Caeli encourages. Calla catches up. Jeremy interrupts with premature applause, *appreciative* applause; they smile and keep on playing. A vocal duet will come later, Madeline taking the lead. Larry will play our miniature piano. The night will go on, and so will these exquisite, enthusing songs—performed for us and for the girls themselves. For winter weather and for friendship. For an evening, sated, satisfied. For no more than that, no less.

The Unbridled Imagination

*S*EVERAL WEEKS AFTER Christmas, on a snowed-in day,
I sit and reread the holiday cards that have collected on
the sill in my office, the news of families I mostly hear
from but once each year. I try to picture the older version of kids I
have not seen since they were small, try to attach the Xeroxed
"Dear all" descriptions to some vague, generalized notion of who
these young people are becoming. There is the *what*, in other
words, and not the *who*. There is the slotting of kids into their categories, the shorthand of the holiday season.

And then a card falls out, a stiff cardboard card, a little
crooked. Written by Caeli, it says. Illustrated by Pascale.
Designed by Lauren. It's a handmade greeting produced by
Karen's kids—a glimpse at the souls of the young. "I put my violin
on the table next to me, and reached for my water bottle," Caeli's
story begins.

I could still hear the melody echoing in my head. It blended with the sound of the chamber choir in the next room.

I twisted off the cap of my water bottle and took a sip, glancing out the window at the busy city. It was late November. I had been wishing for snow, or even just a small frost. My wish had been only partly granted—it was windier outside than it had been all week. Trash was flying through the air like birds. The streetlights lining the road were decorated with snowflake lights, too far in advance, I thought. A small crowd of people—teenagers, women with young children, and old couples—were holding up signs and marching back and forth in front of City Hall.

ATTACK IRAQ? NO! said one sign painted in red.

STOP THE WAR!

LET THERE BE PEACE!

I sighed and put the water bottle back, walking closer to the window. More people were crossing the streets to join the protestors. They had no signs, but American and Iraqi flags glued together, back to back. I put my elbows on the cold windowsill. I was trying to ignore the aching fear inside me. I turned back to my violin and my wire, fold-up music stand, and started to play again.

Madeline burst into the room.

"Hey," she said. "What's up?" She walked over to me and peered out the window. "What's goin' on down there?"

"Protestors," I replied, tucking my violin under my arm.

"Hmm."

The two of us stood watching from the window. The glass was tinted; I don't think they could see us. In any case, they didn't look up. The choir next door was singing louder now. It was the song about angels. There was a big rush of wind. Leaves and garbage swirled around the protestors. And the crowd of pigeons stayed at their feet, fighting for bread crumbs, close to the ground.

Peace, Goodwill.

I LOOK UP and watch the snow continue to quilt the backyard. I remember a day at a diner last fall, when Karen and her girls and Jeremy and I were discussing, over orange crème sodas, some Internet game the girls had been playing. You would have thought they'd been given the key to Candyland, the way Madeline, Caeli, and Calla were going on about this virtual space where kids could engage in some kind of technified make-believe with fictional personae of their own making. It took me awhile to figure out that the whole transaction was done with words—that there were no fancy computer graphics, no MTV-style animation that propelled the game along. It was simply and exclusively about building characters and then letting them loose in an electronic world.

The imagination is not dead. There are parents and teachers, neighbors and friends, brothers and sisters, aunts and uncles, books and games, national commissions, even, that are making room for the dreams children dream, the thoughts children have, the stories children want to tell. The imagination is not dead, and because it isn't, there are kids like Caeli who are watching and weighing the storm clouds through a window, kids like the blue-eyed boy who knocks on a door to ask if it's all right to turn a dream into a tale, kids like the little girl who once sat behind me on a train extolling the virtues of Shakespeare to an elderly friend.

The imagination isn't dead, but if it were as vital and conspicuous and esteemed as it should be, there would be fewer lists when it came to kids, more freedom when it came to schedules, less emphasis on resumes and trophies. There would be more literary magazines in more middle schools, more teachers who find the time to read the unassigned stories students write, more Mr.

Stevers, more Mrs. Hendrixes, more Mrs. Stantons. There would be fewer public-opinion polls that suggest that today's kids do not make the world a better place, fewer reports that deliver the draconian news that writing (and therefore the expressed imagination) is the "most neglected" skill in most classrooms, over most grades, across this country.

And there would be more stories like the story my friend Lisa will tell when the snow stops falling and the whiteness melts away and the garden opens again in early spring. Lisa does her work down in the Asian woods. Sometimes we talk about dividing plants in rainy weather. Sometimes she shows me the purple center of a cream-colored bud. Sometimes she tells me how a plant delivers seeds, but this time I will find Lisa beneath a canopy of leaves, laying down the stone for a patio she designed over the long winter of excessive snow. I will ask her how she has been. She will ask me about me. And then she will tell me a story about her son, a third-grader in a public school, who has fallen, all of a sudden, for poems. He is writing poems, she will tell me, with titles like "The Dream," "Heaven," and "Darkness Away." He is writing poems and reading poems; he has lost his self-consciousness with language.

When I ask her why, Lisa will tell me about a teacher, a Mr. Mendell who, it seems, believes in images and metaphors, in the emotional life and possibilities of great stories and great poems. Over the course of the next few weeks I will hear more about this man, more about how he has engaged even the most reluctant kids in an odyssey of the imagination. I will hear about how he has encouraged his students to write freely—unrestrained by rhyme, unconcerned about "capability," uncensored by fear of embarrassment. He likes vivid descriptions, Mr. Mendell. He likes metaphor and the punch and pull of honest emotion. He is a happy proponent of poetic license, and to his classroom and his own poetry he brings the stuff of passion.

Not only that, but Mr. Mendell is a believer—a *diehard* believer—in reading poetry out loud, even the poems penned by the youngest of poets, the poets still finding their way with dreams and words. Mr. Mendell's belief in the power of the shared poem is so absolute that, at one point in the school year, he will call for the creation of a poetry café at a coffee shop in the middle of a nearby town. It is there that his third-graders and their parents will collect one night and take turns reading the poems they've either written or always loved. It is there that each performer will have a chance to discover or express the poet in herself. The kids will take turns reading their poems at the mike. They will return and read a second poem, perhaps a third. And after all the prepared poetry has been exhausted, the kids will, in Lisa's words, begin to "scribble poems on napkins, composing in a delirium so they could recite again."

In May, I will learn from Lisa that her son, Jake, has asked if it will be all right if he writes his dad a birthday poem, instead of buying him art supplies for a gift. I will learn from Lisa that the poem is all tied up with a satin ribbon and presented as a scroll. For Allan, Lisa's husband, the poem will come as a complete surprise. For Jake, it might be the best gift ever given.

COFFEE

Java.
Hot and steaming.
Warm and tasty.
Bitter or sweet.
Relaxing.
Listening to music.
Slumped down in a chair.
With your eyes closed.
Thinking about . . . coffee.

The cold pouring rain outside.
Waiting in the warm, refreshing inside.
Waiting, waiting.
For what?
A nice cup of java.
When it's gone,
I sit up.
Other people are waiting.
So I decide to leave.
But I remember that I don't have an umbrella.
So . . . I get a cappuccino,
With . . .
A chocolate eclair,
A cinnamon bun,
And . . .
Another cup of coffee.

Would "Coffee" exist had a teacher not begun the year by reading aloud from poems about subways and crystal stairs, if he had not introduced Langston Hughes and Walter Dean Myers along the way, if he had not walked among third-graders and read his own poetry aloud? Would a child be eager to invent in just this way if he had not been so effusively invited to let his thoughts run free upon the page? Would a parent now hold the gift of a poem in his hand, if a coffee shop had not been transformed into a poetry café? Would Lisa be telling me months after this about all the other poems that Jake's now written? I don't know for sure, but I rather doubt it. Mr. Mendell has made a difference, and the imagination lives.

In the Director's Seat

"WHAT WOULD YOU think," I call up the stairs toward Jeremy's room, where he disappeared an hour ago, "if we tried to do the writing club one last time this summer?"

"That would be cool," Jeremy's answer somersaults back my way, a little delayed and slightly muffled.

"Do you think enough kids would come? Would want to?" I stand at the base of the stairs, my elbow on the banister, my chin in my hand, my ear turned, listening. There's a crash and a rustle from the room above. A dragging of something heavy across the carpet.

"I don't know." A grunt. "I know a lot of the kids will be at camp. They're already talking about it at lunch."

"Are there kids you'd like me to send letters to, who haven't come before?"

"Yeah. Probably."

"Can you make a list?"

"Yeah. But later."

"What are you doing, anyway?"

"I'm filming a movie, Mom. I'm busy."

"Can I come up and see?"

"In a little while. I'm busy. Concentrating."

I leave him be. I go to my office, sit down to prepare an invitation for the kids—the kids I know I'll send one to and the kids whom I'll hear about later. We'll put Madeline and Caeli on the list for sure. Anyone who's come in the past. Some kids from the church. A boy Jeremy has been sharing his writing with during English. Whoever else Jeremy decides might see the club as pleasure, not obligation. We'll spend the summer, I think, on thematic writing and critique. On learning how to evaluate one another's work (and one's own) without the burden of excessive negatives. We'll talk about how no one wants to feel bad about their writing; they just want—they always need—to make it better. We'll read about the earliest years of famous writers and write reminiscences of our own, picking up on themes the famous writers have suggested. We'll talk about inventors and inventions and then imagine some of our own. We'll build a literary magazine—design it, name it, lay it out, help each other choose our own best work. We'll . . . and now I hear Jeremy calling my name, and I push back from the computer, walk to the bottom of the stairs.

"You want to see?" he's asking me. A rustle. A rattle.

"See what?"

"The beginning of my movie."

"Sure." I take the steps, two at a time.

WHAT WE HAVE here is Playmobil redux. Everything I thought we'd gradually slipped into boxes and bags has been retrieved from the attic and dumped across Jeremy's turquoise-carpeted floor. The figures and their endless hats. The saloon, the police headquarters, the train station. All the walking canes and snap-on collars and dog leashes and chickens and baskets and coinage and tables and chairs and boats and cars and pots and spoons and trains and desks and miniature computers and knapsacks and the accoutrements of dentistry. "My movie," Jeremy says, when he sees my face.

"Your movie?"

"Well I had to cast it first. Select the props."

"And have you done that?"

"Yes, I have. I've even filmed some. You want to see?"

What's going to happen now, I wonder, but Jeremy points to his computer across the room, invites me to take his chair, and I see the flicker of his first genuine movie. Not a comic strip, not a screenplay, not a story designed to feel like a movie, not something he and his father have concocted together, not the beguiling glimmer of an imagined movie in his eyes, but his very own animated movie, created with a kit I had brought home for his birthday and hoped he would find a way to use. The progressively raised arm of a Playmobil policeman, all shot as stills by the tiny computer-linked digital camera and then concatenated to suggest fluidity. The approach of a grimly attired suspect—one step, another step; you can feel the slow motion behind the manufactured speed. The whole thing is not more than five seconds long. It's not done yet, Jeremy tells me.

"So you've been up here all this time shooting a movie?"

"Um-hmm."

"When did you decide to do that?"

"When I was kicking the ball around outside. I got an idea for a plot."

"It's fabulous, Jer."

"It's just a start."

"Wait 'til Dad sees."

"Yeah. Just wait."

.   .   .

THE NEXT SEVERAL days, then, are given over to the production of movies. Bill helps Jeremy with the technical glitches.
Jeremy does the rest by himself. Within what seems like no time
he's cast a new film on a pirate's sea-worn ship, and this one is
long and complicated, requiring several hundred still photographs that he edits, runs together, scores, and titles. I'll hear
the theme song blaring while I sit here in my office. I'll hear the
sound effects, a cannon's blast. I'll hear him curse an adolescent's
curse when some unknown something doesn't work out right.
When I pop up to see the latest version of the show, I realize that
he's mastered a technology and an art form that I could never
master on my own.

On a crisp day in spring I play hostess to two New York photographers who have come to take my photograph at the behest of a
magazine. Three days ago, the daffodils bloomed. Two days ago,
weirdly, it snowed. Today it's bitter cold and brilliantly sunny.
There's a drift of steely clouds in the distance. I'm not keen on
being photographed—are writers, I ask, obliged to be pretty?—
but I like this photographer and his assistant from the moment that
they knock on my door. I like the way they acclimate to the house
without taking it over, how they connote care when they move
things about. They seem optimistic, despite my brazen lack of
glamour. They struggle between them to make me sparkle, to say
something—anything—that will make me forget my misery before
a lens.

They're here a long time—I am no insta-portrait—and
between Polaroids, light tests, and the rapid fire of the camera, we
speak of many things. Of hobbies and travels. Of a collection of
beakers. Of why my posture alone would keep me out of
Hollywood. We play Emmylou Harris and Norah Jones. We discuss books; the photographer's assistant is a reader. It's spring

break, and Jeremy is home from school, and though he has come downstairs from time to time to visit, he's mostly stayed up in his room. I hear the sounds of his movie firing off as the photographer's camera clicks and clicks. A cannon blast. A nautical tune. The sound of marching feet.

"What's your son doing up there, anyway?" the well-read assistant finally asks.

"Making a movie," I say, between takes.

"A movie? Like, a real movie?" There is immediate fascination.

"On his computer," I say, and then I try to explain: "It's this kit that I bought him, designed for kids. It's . . ." And now I have to use my hands to explain the rest so they stop taking pictures, infinitely more interested in what I'm saying than in any pose I could have struck. "He takes a million still photos of these Playmobil figures—they're like Lego figures? Have you ever seen them?—and then he puts the pictures together, and then, you know, he does the sound effects and then . . ."

But I've said enough. The photographers vanish. They finish whatever roll, whatever pose we've been working on, then take the stairs with youthful strides. "It's a little messy up there," I call after them, unheeded. "It's . . ." And then I think, *Oh, God,* as I remember all the not-good-enough-for-a-photo-shoot clothes that I have hurled over the hallway banister, all the makeup in the bathroom that has the door I did not close, all the stuff on Jeremy's floor, the vacuum cleaner in the hallway. *I cleaned the downstairs,* I want to call after them. The downstairs. *See? How pretty? Did you notice the flowers?* But then I think, *Oh, what the hell. I'm a writer. I'm not supposed to be neat.*

By the time I get up the steps and turn the corner, the photographer and his assistant have already taken their places on Jeremy's floor. They sit Indian style while Jeremy sits slouched on his chair above them, swiveling back and forth, like a true director. They're talking shop, and Jeremy's telling them how he does this, how he makes the Playmobil figures look like they're moving, how he chooses the music, how he designs the titles, what he's hoping to achieve, from both the technical and the artistic perspective. They keep asking him to replay his twenty-eight-second film, and every time he does, they get all lit up, tell him it's amazing, tell him he has talent. Then the photographer starts telling my kid about once watching a special on Steven Spielberg. "You should see that show," he tells Jeremy. "You'd really like it. Maybe your mom can find you a copy."

"That would be cool."

"Because, I don't know, but you remind me of Spielberg. That guy was shooting movies at fifteen."

"I know. I read about him."

"You did? Well then you know what I'm talking about. But you should still get this special, you could probably rent it somewhere. It has actual clips from Spielberg's first movies."

"Very cool."

"And you know what else your mom should do?" the photographer continues, rubbing his head now, turning to see me, and smiling. "She should rent the local movie theater so the whole town can see your movie."

"Ahh! Man! That would be *awe*some." Jeremy gets really excited now. Swivels all the way around in his chair, swivels face forward.

"Yeah. Spielberg's parents did it for him. I remember them saying so in that show. You could charge everyone a couple of dollars, break even. It would be fun."

"*Awe*some," Jeremy says again. "Really awesome."

"Can you show me the movie one more time?" the photographer says.

"Sure," Jeremy says. "Absolutely." He swivels back toward the screen. He punches the keyboard, cues the action.

. . .

I LEAVE MY post in Jeremy's doorway and head downstairs. It's early afternoon, it's been a long day, and soon the photographer and his assistant will be driving two hours home.

Within minutes I'm joined by the photographer, who stands against one wall and shakes his head.

"Do you need more photographs?" I ask, hoping he'll say no.

"Yes. But in a minute," he says. "In a minute. We'll get set up." He doesn't move, just stands here, against the pinstriped kitchen wall, shaking his closely cropped head. "That's an amazing kid up there," he finally says. "Really amazing. That was fun to see."

"It means a lot that you took an interest," I say. "Thank you for that. It made our—well, it made more than our day."

"Are you kidding? That was fantastic. I really like your son."

"I could tell he liked talking to you."

"My assistant's still up there. He'll probably be there for a while."

"That's all right."

"I think he's jealous of Jeremy's software."

"That's funny. With all the equipment you carry."

"You know when I was up there," the photographer continues, "I started thinking about who I was, as a kid, what I did with my time. I don't know. Talking to Jeremy kind of made me wonder what would have happened if I'd taken a few more risks, been a little more—I don't know—*original,* maybe, not always sticking with the crowd, not so mainstream."

"But you're a photographer," I say, laughing. "You couldn't have been *that* mainstream."

"Let's just say I put my Legos away earlier than I should have," he says. "I wish, looking back, that I'd made a movie."

"Jeremy would love to hear you say that," I say.

"He's a really great kid," the photographer says.

"I'll tell him," I say. "What you've said, I mean," and I cannot say anything else, I cannot tell this man what his words mean to me. I could never explain, even if he had the time to listen, about all the questions I have carried in my head, all the rules I know I've broken, all the faith, the sometimes lonely faith, I have placed in the imagination. I could never explain, but this man who looks through a lens for a living does not need me to. He has sat on the floor in my son's messy room and caught a glimpse of the future.

Postscript

EDNESDAY, JUST BEFORE dusk. A pause in the day. The butterfly balloon we've named Bella is perched in the corner of one room, and Grunt, the balloon frog, glints with violet optimism. The smell of Casablanca lilies permeates the house, and there is the drone of bees in a nearby hive and more birds than I remember. Earlier this afternoon, a deer stood alert on the lawn and did not stir, even as I crossed the path toward her.

Something is different this year; something has changed. The kids come earlier and linger longer, and often, now, the parents will stay afterwards to talk, to tell me the stories behind the stories that the kids have started to write. In my couches, on my floor, near my garden, on my deck, things are being written that both break and heal my heart. The raw poetry of adolescence. The fearless juxtaposition of oversized words. The tonic of laughter as one borrows a detail, as two barter with memory, as three stake out a space on the front stoop to craft the opening of a play. I ask to see the room in which an inventor works, and Madeline gives me a curtain that rises, a "large, metallic-looking room," and "several stainless-steel chairs and countless lemons hanging from ropes of wire attached to the ceiling." I ask to be taken into the mind of a girl named Paloma, and Greta walks me right into the house where the character lives, where roof tiles are "coming undone like a baby tooth hanging from a thread" and windows "have cracks thin like strands of silk." I want to know if Daniel can imagine how John must have felt when John, while reading his book, was struck by a pickup truck, and Daniel writes, as Daniel will, of a "demonic engine" coming like a "dark avatar" out of "the twisting nether." Sophie writes of a street that wheels in an endless circle and Anya of a street that replays itself like a strip of film, and Sarah unearths the treasures of her own neighborhood while Caeli muses over plastic statuettes on lawns. Tiernan's character will notice that a number of an address has fallen, "leaving a faded silhouette against the peeling, crimson paint." Gabrielle will write of "a single tear" on a character's face. Stephen will tell the story of a wrongly named child, and Jeremy will write of children caught in the trenches of war. When I ask the kids to reflect on the work that they have heard, Jake will be the first, every single time, to raise his hand with effusive, eager praise.

Wednesday, and the light is nearly gone from the sky, and soon the cars will roll down this street and the doors will bang and the music I've been playing softly will be stilled. I will read out loud and urge and commission, and the kids will write for themselves and one another. It will grow perfectly dark but we will lose all track of time, and there will be no judge among us. Only the imagination, that's all, and wherever it might take us.

Appendix One

A few years ago I stood in a classroom in a public elementary school and began reading aloud to fourth-grade kids. The kids and I have been learning together ever since about what makes for fun in an after-school or summer program and about what animates and nurtures, prompts and evokes. Throughout my time with these students and with others, I have tried to remember the ways in which I myself have been encouraged to see beyond the obvious and to write better than before.

Of course, I never know for certain whether an exercise or reading might work until I present it to the kids, and sometimes I find myself changing an exercise midcourse, taking my cues from the expressions on their faces. When something is working, I let it spin itself out into unforeseen directions. When something impedes or distracts, I cut it short. The first rule and the last rule are to open doors, not close them. To honor the fragile beginnings.

The suggestions that follow are suggestions only, a starting place. There are countless resources for those who wish to build a bigger teaching platform or to muse over what it is that we do when we sit down to encourage stories and story making. One of my favorites is the two-volume series *Educating the Imagination: Essays and Ideas for Teachers and Writers*, a Teachers & Writers Collaborative publication edited by Christopher Edgar and Ron Padgett. The TWC Web site (www.twc.org), with its wealth of links, publications, and suggested exercises (some of which have most certainly inspired some of my own teaching), is enormously helpful as well. I also suggest spending some time on the National Writing Project Web site (www.writingproject.org) to learn more about the opportunities and texts available to those who make it their business to build the imagination. For a thoughtful appraisal of the status of writing in the nation's classrooms, visit the official Web site of the National Commission on Writing (www.writingcommission.org).

Other books that instruct, direct, and clarify: *The Call of Stories: Teaching and the Moral Imagination*, that indispensable classic by Robert Coles; *The Situation and the Story: The Art of Personal Narrative*, by Vivian Gornick; *The Writer's Block: 786 Ideas to Jump-Start Your Imagination*, by Jean Rekulak; "The Autobiography Box: A Step-by-Step Kit for Examining the Life Worth Living," by Brian Bouldrey; *I Could Tell You Stories: Sojourns in the Land of Memory*, by Patricia Hampl; *How to Read a Poem: and Fall in Love with Poetry*, by Edward Hirsch; and, of course, *Bird by Bird: Some Instructions on Writing and Life*, by Anne Lamott and *On Writing: A Memoir of the Craft*, by Stephen King.

I am a parent, not a certified teacher. The exercises suggested here can, with just a few modifications, fill a rainy afternoon or a muggy summer day for one's own child or children. At the same time, they can form the centerpiece of activities played out among cousins, friends, neighbors, and classmates. The point, in the end, is to have the conversation. To make room for setting young minds free.

Sample Workshop Activities

Fourth / Fifth Grades

Session One

Theme: Irony and Trick Endings
Readings: "The Invisible Child," by Tove Jansson
           "The Ransom of Red Chief," by O. Henry
(Both tales can be found in *Children's Classics to Read Aloud*, selected by Edward Blishen.)

Suggestions: After discussing the textbook meaning of irony as well as the role irony plays in everyday life, ask the kids to think back on their past week and identify the most ironic things that happened. Have them write a short description of their turn with irony and ask those who wish to share their stories to read them out loud to the others.

Now read aloud from "The Invisible Child." Ask the kids to raise their hands every time they think they hear an ironic statement. Ask why the author might be using irony at that moment. Ask how the story would be different if the author had avoided irony altogether.

Now talk about the concept of trick endings. Ask the kids to tell you about other favorite stories with trick endings. After each of the kids has had a chance to contribute, read "The Ransom of Red Chief" all the way up through the part when the kidnappers of the troublesome boy decide to write the boy's father a letter. Ask the kids to write their own trick letter here—to turn the tables on the tale somehow in a way that might not have been expected. Give the kids fifteen minutes, then ask that they read their respective letters to the others. Then finish reading O. Henry's tale and discuss the impact of his own trick ending.

Session Two

Theme: Alternative Realities

Reading: "Sindbad the Sailor," from *Ali Baba and the Forty Thieves and Other Stories*, published by Derrydale

Materials: Stiff cardboard, colored pens and pencils, die, poker chips or coins that might be used as game-board markers

Suggestions: "Sindbad the Sailor" is the story a wealthy voyager named Sindbad tells to a poor porter (named Hindbad) about the "greatest mental and bodily sufferings" endured during the seven voyages that brought him to his current station in life.

As you read the story aloud to the kids, ask them to consider a series of *What might have happened if?* questions. What might have happened if Sindbad, during his first voyage, had escaped with the others on the boat after the "island" they were standing on proved to be the back of a whale? What might have happened if, on the second voyage, Sindbad had not fallen asleep beneath the tree?

Following that discussion, divide the kids into small groups and ask them to invent a game (and to build a corresponding game board) that establishes the choices or opportunities that might befall an imaginary adventurer. What are some of the various paths that the adventurer might take? How would his or her life be affected by choosing one path over another?

Session Three

Theme: Reporting versus Storytelling
Reading: *Call It Courage,* by Armstrong Sperry

Suggestions: Ask the kids to read the novel *Call It Courage* prior to coming to the workshop. Open the session with a discussion about their reactions to this story concerning a young island boy who has lived in fear of the sea since he lost his mother to it. Ask the kids to define *courage*. Ask them to consider whether they, like the hero, Mafatu, would have felt the need to prove to themselves that they are, in fact, brave.

Then ask the kids to turn to the final pages of the book, in which Mafatu, having gone off on his own on a perilous ocean journey, struggles to make his way home. Ask the kids to consider how the story might have been told by a journalist standing on the shoreline, watching the boy struggling with the seas. How would the journalist render the scene? Whom might the journalist interview to broaden the perspective? Ask the kids to write the headline and the first three paragraphs. After the kids have read their work aloud, talk about the differences between reporting and storytelling.

Session Four

Theme: Adjectives
Reading: "Rikki-Tikki-Tavi," by Rudyard Kipling

Suggestions: Open the session with a discussion about nouns, verbs, adjectives, and adverbs, and how each might be used to good effect. Have the kids make lists of their favorite adjectives and adverbs and ask them why those words work so well in stories.

Then ask the kids to pull out a fresh piece of paper and get ready to catch as many adjectives as they can while you read them the Kipling story "Rikki-Tikki-Tavi." After you've finished reading the story, discuss the many ethical questions that it prompts: Can the words *good* and *bad* be applied to animals? Who has the stronger claim to a garden: a mongoose or a snake? Can a mongoose be the hero of the story if he does too many questionable things? Then ask the kids to return to their lists of adjectives. Ask them to circle the best adjectives that they jotted down and to write a poem incorporating as many of those words as they can.

Session Five

Theme: Evocative Writing
Reading: *The Family Under the Bridge,* by Natalie Savage
Carlson

Suggestions: Ask the kids to read the novel *The Family Under the Bridge* before coming to the session. Spend time talking with them about the moral implications of this tale about the homeless hobo who is forced to share his spot under the bridge with a poor mother and her three children. Talk about how chance encounters can change lives forever, and how the hobo himself recognizes that when he says, "Now that he had befriended these starlings, his life would never again be completely his own."

Then ask the kids to talk to you about their favorite descriptions of place in the book. Which sentences are the most evocative? Why? Which sentences make them feel as if they are there, with the family under the bridge? Ask the kids to write a paragraph or poem about their favorite hiding places, using some of the same evocative techniques the author uses in this novel. Ask for volunteers to read the original pieces aloud.

Sixth / Seventh Grades

Session One

Theme: Word Fun

Readings: "The Old Gumbie Cat," by T. S. Eliot

      "Stopping by Woods on a Snowy Evening," by Robert Frost

      "The Raven," by Edgar Allan Poe

Recordings: *Poetry Speaks: Hear Great Poets Read Their Work from Tennyson to Plath,* edited by Elise Paschen and Rebekah Presson Mosby

Suggestions: After reading from the classic poems, open the discussion by asking the kids to define just what a poem is. Introduce them to the terminology of poetry—meter, assonance, stanzas, rhymes, enjambed lines, end-stopped lines. Remind them that the basic unit of all poetry is the word, and that good poetry arises from a familiarity with (and love for) words.

Ask the kids to write down some of their favorite words. Ask them to make sure they have some verbs, some nouns, a few colors, a few places, a few adverbs, and at least one proper name. (Variations of this exercise have been posted on the TWC Web site.) Once the kids have two-dozen or so words on their lists, ask them to swap their lists with their near neighbors. Then ask the kids to use this raw material—these lists of a neighbor's favorite words—to fashion a short poem. Ask them to use at least ten words from the list they have been given.

Now have the kids read their poems out loud so that you and the others might help them identify the very best line that they have written thus far. That best line now becomes the first and last line of a brand new poem.

Now give the kids a single line—I've used "Beneath the light of a timid moon"—and ask them to begin a poem with it. After they've read aloud from the poems they've written, encourage them to consider how it is that the same seven words could provoke so many responses.

You might wish to end the poetry session by dimming the lights and playing chosen recordings from the extraordinary volume *Poetry Speaks*—a book and CD collection that features the work of Walt Whitman, Robert Frost, William Carlos Williams, T. S. Eliot, and many more as read by the poets themselves. Provide the kids with Xeroxes of the poems that are being read so that they can follow along. It's often interesting to ask the kids to read the poems out loud first—before they hear them being read by the authors—and then to discuss how the authors' own intonations and inflections give new meaning to the works.

Session Two

Theme: Telling an Interesting Story
Reading: "Casey at the Bat," by Ernest Thayer

Suggestions: After reading "Casey at the Bat," ask the kids to reflect on what makes the story itself so interesting. How does the author tell us what the conflict is? How does telling the story through the vehicle of a poem build tension and interest? How do the repeated rhythms establish momentum? Ask the kids to tell you whether the poem is satisfying to them. Ask them which phrases feel most powerful and engaging.

Next read a list of recent headlines. I used "Terror at Dusk," "Behind the Smile," "Body of Evidence," "The Split Personality," "The Art of Reflection," "Preppy with a Punch," "Taking the Long View," "World Music," and "Pitch Perfect." Ask the kids to choose their favorite three headlines and to develop corresponding plot synopses. What might make these abbreviated stories interesting if the kids were to develop them? What kind of language and pacing might sustain interest in the reader to the very end? How might they turn their stories into "Casey at the Bat"–like poems to further develop their power?

Now show the kids five photographs of very different faces. Ask them to choose a face and to imagine a problem that person might be facing. Ask the kids to write a paragraph that describes the problem in a way that is provocative and interesting. Ask them to convert that paragraph into a poem.

Session Three

Theme: Beginnings
Readings: The opening pages of *Tom Sawyer,* by Mark Twain
The opening pages of *The Hobbit,* by J.R.R. Tolkein

Suggestions: As you read aloud from the opening pages of these stories, ask the kids to consider what the beginnings promise about the stories to come. Ask them to reflect on the tools the respective authors use to establish character and conflict. Talk about point of view—I focus on first-person and third-person discussions at this age—and how the chosen point of view affects the nature of the story that will be told.

Now ask the kids to imagine a zoo in winter, a miserly old zookeeper, and a lost little girl. Ask them to imagine some sort of conflict arising from these elements and to write the story from the first-person point of view of the zookeeper. Ask them to read aloud from their work.

Now ask the kids to write the story from the first-person point of view of the little girl. Ask the kids to talk about what happens to their stories as they reversed the point of view.

Now ask the kids to give these two same characters an entirely different problem to solve and to write a story in the third person about what happens.

Session Four

Theme: Character Development

Readings: The opening pages of *The Old Man and the Sea,* by Ernest Hemingway

The opening pages of *Bud, Not Buddy,* by Christopher Paul Curtis

Suggestions: Ask the kids to think about just how Hemingway and Curtis help us learn who their characters are. What do we know, even early on, about contradictions or dreams or frustrations? What is memorable or interesting about the way the characters have been described?

Now ask the kids to sketch out five or six characters of their own by pairing an imaginary character with an unexpected trait. For example: The portly grocer . . . sleeps in his truck. The little girl won't speak . . . but she loves to blow bubbles. The old baseball player lost two fingers . . . but still plays a mean game of pool.

Now have the kids develop their characters. Ask them to consider questions such as, How does this character walk? How does he/she use his/her hands when he/she talks? What are the noticeable speech patterns (southern accent? English as a second language?)? Was this character loved as a child? Did something traumatic happen early on? What does this character own, crave, and do for a living?

After the kids have named a number of additional attributes for each of the characters, ask them to choose their favorite fictional concoction and to write a five-paragraph story about him or her.

Session Five

Theme: Dialogue
Readings: Excerpts from *A Room with a View,* by E. M. Forster
Excerpts from *Housekeeping,* by Marilynne Robinson

Suggestions: Ask the kids to listen to the way the characters speak to each other in the chosen stories. What does the sound of their talk tell us about them (that is, What part of the world are they from? What kind of education might they have been given? Are they timid or bold, aggressive or bored? Can they be trusted? Are they credible?)? How does the author use dialogue to advance the story, to reveal underlying tensions, and to provide information?

Now ask the kids to imagine themselves sitting in a cave on a stormy night, waiting out the rain. Suddenly two men appear on the other side of the hideout. The interlopers begin to dig in the earth and to talk to each other, unaware that any eavesdropping is going on. Write a story around the conversation that passes between these two unseen men. What can be suggested about the men—their age, their education, their moral stance, their ambitions, their vulnerabilities, their relationship to each other—through dialogue alone?

Eighth / Ninth Grades

Note: As the kids get older and assimilate the many elements of the craft, it is important to provide them with the tools they'll need to critique their own work as well as the work of others. At this age, I restructure the workshop sessions to provide more room for group discussion. I steer the kids away from making definitive statements about good or bad and frame the critique of every piece around the following four questions:

What mood does the story provoke?

What details are particularly effective and evocative?

What does the chosen point of view allow the author to accomplish, and how does the point of view also limit or thwart the story?

What questions have been raised by this draft that might be answered in a subsequent reworking?

Session One

Theme: The Inventive Mind

Readings: *Mr. McMurtry's Bubble Hat and Other Great Moments in American Ingenuity: More than 50 Oddball Inventions from the Annals of the U.S. Patent Office,* by Mike Miller

> *The Picture History of Great Inventors,* by Gillian Clements

> Excerpts from *Our Town,* by Thornton Wilder

> Excerpts from *Inherit the Wind,* by Jerome Lawrence and Robert E. Lee

> Excerpts from *Death of a Salesman,* by Arthur Miller

> Excerpts from *The Cherry Orchard,* by Anton Chekhov

Suggestions: *Mr. McMurtry's Bubble Hat* provides a humorous glimpse at some of the more unusual ideas put forth by American inventors—everything from a milker's mask (to protect the milker's face from the whisk of a cow's tail) to a cable harness system that can tether ocean bathers to the shore, to an alarm clock that might be wired directly into a busy man's ears so that he can be awakened on time without disturbing the sleep of others. This is a fun book to review in concert with *The Picture History of Great Inventors,* which provides an illustrated look at some better-known inventions and inventors.

After reviewing the inventions with the kids, ask them to make a list of the top-five inventions of all time. Ask them to share their lists with you and the others and then to suggest the most important thing that has not yet been invented.

Now ask the kids to imagine that their not-yet-invented invention has finally emerged in the world. Ask them to imagine that Eureka moment of invention, the character of the inventor, and the character of the inventor's assistant. I like to use work sheets that help spur the kids' imaginations by asking such questions as, Where is the inventor when the breakthrough occurs? What time of day is it? What sort of mood did the inventor wake up in? What is the inventor's relationship with his/her assistant? How long have they been working toward this invention? What has the inventor's life been like up until this point?

Next read chosen scenes from the four plays listed above and lead the kids in a discussion about the structure and components of a successful play. Talk through how the playwrights establish their settings, how dialogue is used to develop character, how stage directions play a role in illuminating plot, character, and action. Divide the kids into groups of three and ask them to jointly develop an inventor, an invention, and a Eureka moment, all within the context of one short dramatic scene.

Session Two

Theme: What's in a Name?

Reading: Excerpts from *The Namesake,* by Jhumpa Lahiri

Suggestions: Jhumpa Lahiri's first novel does an extraordinary job of tracing the consequences that arise when a Bengali baby is given the unusual Russian name Gogol. Not knowing at first where the odd name comes from, the namesake finds himself humiliated one day when a high-school teacher tells the life story of the mentally unstable writer Gogol. It is this humiliation that provides a turning point for the protagonist of Lahiri's book.

After reading the pertinent sections of the novel, assign each kid a separate name, along with its respective meaning. I have used the *Dictionary of First Names,* by Alfred Kolatch, to help me here, and I have used such names as the following:

Boys' Names
Ivan "grace"
Clark "learned man"
Alan "harmony, peace"
Denis "wild, frenzied"
Strom "a bed, a mattress"
Logan "a felled tree"
Clement "gentle, merciful"

Girls' Names
Sudy "from the south"
Patience "to suffer"
Blythe "happy"
Paloma "dove"

Kirsten "church"
Miriam "sea of bitterness, sorrow"
Alouise "famous in battle"
Frieda "peace"

Now ask the kids to write a two-part story that takes its inspiration from the assigned names. For the first part of the story, ask the kids to imagine the day when the protagonist discovers the story behind his/her name—what it means and why it was chosen for him/her. Where is Miriam, for example, when she is finally told why she was named what she was named? Who tells her? What is her reaction? What does the conversation sound like?

For the second part of the story, ask the kids to imagine how their protagonists are changed by the knowledge they have been given about their names. Do they begin to change certain behaviors in order to be more like a Miriam? Do they rename themselves with a nickname in an effort to shed the uncomfortable or unwanted associations of the name? Do they tell others about their name with pride, or is it a secret they attempt to keep to themselves? And how does the relationship between Miriam and the person who has told her the story of her name grow or change in the aftermath of their conversation? Do they trust each other more? Are they wary of each other?

Note: In volume two of *Educating the Imagination*, Elizabeth Radin Simons provides another interesting approach to the naming theme in her chapter entitled "The Folklore of Naming."

Session Three

Theme: Gainfully Employed
Reading: "Bus Problems," by Howard Norman
(This can be found in the collection *When I Was Your Age: Original Stories about Growing Up,* volume two, edited by Amy Ehrlich.)

Suggestions: In "Bus Problems," Howard Norman tells what happened to him in the summer of 1959, when he worked as an assistant to the local librarian and driver of the bookmobile. Everything seemed perfectly normal and calm until, on an ordinary afternoon, Howard Norman found his bookmobile to be the center of police activity.

After reading Norman's essay aloud, ask the kids to write about their first volunteer (or paid) responsibility and all the things that might have gone (or actually did go) wrong. Encourage the kids to use evocative descriptions, well-chosen adjectives, and pointed dialogue to create two or three telling scenes. Why did they want the job in the first place? What did they think it would be like? Whom did they work with? What surprised them? If everything went perfectly well, what might have gone wrong? If something disastrous did occur, what happened, could it have been prevented, and what was the final resolution? What, in the end, was learned from the experience?

Session Four

Theme: Science Fair

Readings: Excerpts from *The Center of Everything*, by Laura
        Moriarty

Excerpts from *We Were There, Too!: Young People in
U.S. History*, by Phillip Hoose

Suggestions: Laura Moriarty's coming-of-age novel is graced
with an exquisite scene in which the young heroine attends a
statewide science fair. Phillip Hoose's history book is a fabulous
collection of stories about kids who played critical roles in
American history.

After reading selected excerpts from the books, ask the kids
to remember the top-five critical junctures in their own lives—
turning points they'll never forget: a science fair; a musical performance; a moment on the soccer field; a speech before the
student body; a day they helped save the life of a kitten; the day
a brother was born. Ask them to define what was so life changing
about the moment. Ask them if they realized something important was happening at the time, or if they only realized this in
retrospect.

Now pair the kids into groups of two and ask them to interview one another about those critical junctures. Ask them to collect enough details so that the interviewer might write of the
interviewee's turning point with conviction and clarity. What was
the person wearing when the event occurred? Whom was she
with? Was it raining or snowing? What time of day was it? What
thoughts went through his mind? How did the moment affect her

sense of self? Did he keep any artifacts from that day and put them away in a treasured box or corner of his room? Did she ever tell anyone about the moment, or did she keep it to herself? When the interviews are finalized, ask each kid to write a first-person essay that stands him/her in the other's shoes.

Tenth / Eleventh / Twelfth Grades

Session One

Theme: The Original Mind

Suggestions: According to Richard Lederer in his book *The Miracle of Language*, computer studies have suggested that it would take ten trillion years to "utter all the possible English sentences that use exactly twenty words."

This extraordinary claim can be partly proved by the kids themselves. Bring a painting or postcard to the workshop and give the students time to interpret the artwork in precisely twenty words. Encourage them to read their work aloud and to compare their interpretations against those of the others.

Having thereby made your case that there is still an infinite number of untold stories left to write and tell in the world, present the kids with a shell, a clove of garlic, a penny, and a rose petal—or any artifacts of your choosing. Ask them to choose the article that resonates most deeply with them and to write a story about what happened when they encountered one of those objects at one point in time.

Session Two

Theme: Abbreviated Lives

Suggestions: In August of 1994, Bill, Jeremy, and I traveled to Spoleto, Italy, so that I might attend a writers' workshop conducted by Reginald Gibbons and Rosellen Brown. It was my first exposure to Italian hill towns and Italian nuns, my first time hearing opera sung from the pulpit of an Italian church, and my first time in the company of writers.

Spoleto was, for me, a revelation: about how the right readings can dislodge the right questions, how the right suggestions can salvage a broken sentence, how the right exercises can unspool entire, unexpected journeys into the imagination. Reginald and Rosellen created a safe place in which to try out tenses, plots, personae. They created an environment in which writers learned to transcend themselves—to see history in a street or face, to imagine the lives marked by tombstones.

I like to give the older kids one of the exercises that Rosellen and Reginald suggested in Spoleto—to conjure up an entire life out of a name on a tombstone, the birth and death dates, and a brief tribute. The following (fictional) tombstone entries might be used to prompt the exercise.

b. 1901 d. 1904
Anna Grace Smith
She was a bird, flying off before we knew her.

b. 1929 d. 1999
Giovanni D'Imperio
Here Giovanni lies, still resting.

b. 1928 d. 1944
Anthony Mark
He died for us.

b. 1952 d. 1969
Melissa Drinker
Gone but not forgotten.

b. 1971 d. 1979
Matthew DeBorg
He returns to the angels.

Session Three

Theme: The Unmasked Self

Readings: Excerpts from *Limbo: A Memoir*, by A. Manette Ansay

Excerpts from *American Chica: Two Worlds, One Childhood*, by Marie Arana

Excerpts from *An American Childhood*, by Annie Dillard

Excerpts from *Misgivings: My Mother, My Father, Myself*, by C. K. Williams

Suggestions: As you read aloud from these classic texts, remind the kids that memoir writing involves the shaping of a life and not the mere recording of it—that a catalog of events and descriptions will not be interesting to anyone but the writer.

Then ask the kids to remember a room in a house from long ago. Ask them to make a list of all the things that come to mind. The furniture. The scuff marks. The ornaments. The quality of the sun. The hiss of radiators. The smells. Where the cat slept, the clumps of hair the cat left behind. How the drawers were arranged. What the doors led to. What was continually lost in the shelves. What conversations were overhead. Give the kids ten minutes to come up with a catalogue of remembered facts.

Now ask the kids to reflect on who they were when they first encountered that room—what the going concerns or joys of their lives were back then. Ask them to write an essay in the present tense that captures a moment in remembered time.

Session Four

Theme: Place as Poetry

Readings: Prologue from *A Death in the Family,* by James Agee

Excerpts from *The House on Mango Street,* by Sandra Cisneros

Excerpts from *The Journey Home,* by Olaf Olafsson

Excerpts from *This Side of Brightness,* by Colum McCann

Excerpts from *Seeing Through Places: Reflections on Geography and Identity,* by Mary Gordon

Suggestions: As you read the excerpts out loud to the kids, ask them to keep a running tally of the phrases that allow them to see what the writer is describing. Ask them to draw what the writer has helped them to see—to translate the words into a picture. Ask them to share their work with the others in the room.

Now ask the kids to consider the impact of place on mood, memories, ideas, and dreams. Ask them to develop an essay around one of the following prompts:

- The physical landscape of their first remembered vacation
- The sounds and smells of an underground rail or subway station
- A place they were not meant to see
- The house they would like to live in and why

Session Five

Theme: Other Touchstone Exercises

Suggestions: In addition to the writing exercises described above, I have found that the following exercises tend to elicit wonderful stories from kids of all ages:

Empty the things in your pockets or your pocketbook and think about what they suggest. Does your comb make you think of your first haircut or your mother's hands? Does your pocket change make you remember your first job around the house? Does your jewelry remind you of family gift-giving traditions? What do things in your pockets and jewelry boxes tell you about the life you have been living?

Go into the kitchen while your mother or father is cooking and close your eyes. What do you smell? What do you hear? What do the sounds and smells remind you of in terms of family meals or stolen treats or holidays or private conversations you had with your dad or mom? What do the smells and sounds of your kitchen tell you about the life you have been living?

Go through the family photo albums and look through the pictures. What do you see? What do the photographs tell you about what the photographer thought was important—for example, does your father photograph you only when you are doing something funny and your mother photograph you only when you are all dressed up? What do the photographs tell you about yourself— are you comfortable being photographed? What do the photographs tell you about the life you have been living?

Make a list of all the holidays you remember living through and write down the details you remember—where you were, who was there with you, what was celebrated in a solemn way, what was merely silly, what you wore, what you ate, presents that were exchanged. What does the way you celebrate your life tell you about the life you have been living?

Go to your favorite hiding place—the basement, the tree out back, the attic. Take notice of all the details—the light, the shapes, the artifacts, the distance from other people. What do the details of your favorite hiding place tell you about the life you have been living?

After the kids have crafted their first draft, ask them to study what they have created. What do they have? Have they chosen all the best details? Are some details missing that should be included and are others included that don't help advance the story? Does the text feel essentially true? Would the text interest them if someone else had written it? Is the voice right? Are they telling the story with the best voice, the best perspective? If, for example, their essay is about what they learned from an experience, are they telling the story in a voice that lets the reader know that time has passed? If the story is about how they saw the world when they were younger, does that younger self come alive in the prose?

Appendix Two

LITERATURE WITH FLAIR: YOUTH WRITING 2003

In the summer of 2003, thirteen kids gathered on six consecutive Wednesday nights and gave free rein to their imaginations—reading, writing, and partnering on dramatic scenes, interactive dialogues, movie scenarios, and prose. On their last evening together, they read through their collected works, gently edited here and there, and brought the stories to life with illustrations. This is the product of their spirited collaboration.

On Inventors and Inventions

After reading about some very silly patent applications, we talked about the five best things ever invented and the five best things that have not been invented yet. John decided that what the world needs now is a way to get to Mars, and here he gives a persuasive accounting of just how we all might get there:

> *How would you like to live on Mars? Well with this inven-*
> *tion, you can. It's a set of generators (28" x 28") that creates*
> *an atmosphere and generates oxygen. With this invention*
> *we can colonize other planets such as Mars. But you can not*
> *have only one generator a planet. It depends on the size of*
> *the planet; a planet the size of Mars might need at least*
> *twenty. And they must be spread out, because if they were*
> *placed side-by-side the planet wouldn't be able to sustain*
> *life. Why? Because the oxygen will still escape into space*
> *and the one spot of atmosphere doesn't protect the planet*
> *from the matter out in space. With this invention we can*
> *advance scientifically. This will be one huge step forward*
> *for mankind.*
>
> > *By John*

We then read from the opening pages of *Death of a Salesman*, *Our Town*, and *Inherit the Wind* and talked about scenes and settings in plays. Next we divided into groups. Each group chose an invention to write about and conjured up the background against which the play's opening scene would take place.

> *As the curtain rises, the audience takes in a large metallic-*
> *looking room furnished with several stainless-steel chairs*
> *and countless lemons hanging from ropes of wire attached*
> *to the ceiling. Some lemons have slits cut in them and are*
> *dripping glistening juice.*
>
> > *By Madeline*

> *His lab was a large room. It was shaped like a dome. The*
> *floor and the wallpaper were white. Most objects were*

either brown or white. The door could only open with fin-
gerprint ID. To the right of the door was a drawer for the
safety equipment, and this was next to another drawer.
That drawer contained the chemicals that were used to cre-
ate various food products. Those food products were made
on the table next to the cabinets that contained the food,
and this is where the products were put.

By Jeremy

Now, still working together, we developed dialogue sequences
between the inventor and his assistant. This is a dialogue developed
by Jeremy and Jake. The invention at issue is designed to turn foods
that are unhealthy but taste good into completely healthy foods:

Jeremy's Inventor: Remember my thought about sugar?
Jake's Assistant: No. Refresh my memory.
JI: I asked, Why are the best foods in life the least healthy?
JA: Because sugars, fats, and oils sweeten but the body dis-
    likes them.
JI: Well, well, well, That will change.
JA: It's impossible.
JI: Not in my mind (picks up a liquid). Do you know what
    this is?
JA: Looks like nitroglycerin. Are you going to blow up the
    sugar factories?
JI: No, but you are on the right track. Take a snack food, for
    example, popcorn. Put this liquid into the popcorn. Then
    when you eat the popcorn, you will still get the same
    great taste but once the popcorn is digested the fats and
    oils leave your body.
JA: Sounds like a fantasy. It goes against the principles of
    food. You should see a psychiatrist.
JI: Well, well, well. Just wait and see.

On Neighborhoods

We read aloud from *Coming Through Slaughter, The House on Mango Street,* and *This Side of Brightness* and discussed how writers create a sense of history, color, rhythm, and sound in their descriptions of place. We then wrote about our own neighborhoods.

Riding along in a car, passing a fence so close to the road it's like trying to get through a crack in a door. As you go along the street you pass houses with beautiful gardens and then you come suddenly to a dead end. So you turn around and see everything again like you are watching a movie and then rewinding it. And then off you go onto the busy road you came from.

By Anya

No one drives down our lonely street. An occasional expensive SUV may drive down the cul-de-sac accidentally, making a wrong turn. The homes are old and large with shaded windows like half-lidded eyes. The homes used to be part of a horse show. Some of them are rustic barns. Although the horse show has been moved, some of the pieces of history still remain. Glass bottle shards glint and twinkle merrily in the sun hidden by thick green grass. A crumbling stone pigpen hidden in an expanse of maples is now where people dispose of unwanted garbage. As the wind blows through the treetops and the opened windows the whole street seems to sigh.

By Sarah

The circle is filled by houses all looking like each other. The hill starts rising in the middle like a ski lift to the top of a mountain. The stream flows almost like nothing down the lower side. It is never completely filled, only half empty or half full like a glass of water. Deer walk through the streets as if there is no ending. But that's true, there is no ending. It's a circle, it keeps on turning and turning and turning.

By Sophie

My neighborhood is located off to the side of a busy, winding church road. The faded gray street of my neighborhood passes by a dozen or so houses stopping at a large cul-de-sac. The houses themselves have the appearance of having been there for at least ten years, and the street and curb are very worn out. The lawns are all very well kept and are each different shades of healthy greens. The materials of which the houses are made vary from faded red and brown bricks to smooth tan stones and cream stucco. Every window on the street is shuttered, and the gardens are neat and tidy. Many of the beds contain lovely yellow day lilies and other such flowers, while from others sprout shrubs. If you had the misfortune to walk down my street on a very hot day, you would find little shade, for many of the big leafy trees are in the back of the houses. On such an afternoon there is little noise because everyone is confining themselves to their air-conditioned homes. All you might hear is the roar of a lawn mower or the splash of a person jumping into the cold waters of their pool. My street is just like any other suburban neighborhood except for the fact that it is my home.

By Gabrielle

Walk up the hill from the church with the withering daisies on its grass. You'll pass the sawdusty playground from which the clanging of the bell repeats over and over. Soon you'll be by the bar without a name next to the small building that seems to have no purpose. Ivy has grown all over the bluish door, making you uncertain whether or not the small, rusty, metal object sticking out from behind the plant is its handle. Farther up the hill is the hardware store with the unrelated objects displayed in the window, such as dark red guitars and that rocket ship trash can that has never been sold. The houses, which are mostly twins, have little gardens in front of them.

By Caeli

Cars rush by, the speeding bullets Superman is faster than. Every Sunday, lawn mowers and other forms of lawn-improving machinery can be heard uttering their loud growl. A train will pass, a metal thunderstorm, rattling windows and sending dogs barking. A basketball is often heard bouncing on the silent wind. Bikes' tires create a sub-tle hum as they go by, and the occasional motor scooter roars by. The middle-class bourgeoisie is oblivious in the spacious yet medium-sized homes, except for the one on the hill, a shining comet in a pantheon of dead stars.

By Daniel

Placing Fictional Characters into Actual Settings

After writing about our own neighborhoods, we developed fictional characters and transplanted them into the neighborhoods that we had earlier described. Working in groups of two or three, we developed dialogue sequences that brought the fictional characters to life and into some kind of confrontation with one another. This is what happens when Jeremy's character arrives in Daniel's neighborhood.

> *Daniel's Character: I see you're new to this area.*
> *Jeremy's Character: I am. Louder than expected.*
> *DC: You sure are.*

JC: *I like it here. There was too little going on in my old neighborhood in New Jersey.*

DC: *Yes. It's very nice here. I've lived here for thirty-two years.*

JC: *Thirty-two years! Has much changed since then?*

DC: *Not really. This place is just more hi-tech. New people, too. That's about it.*

JC: *It's definitely high tech. Some of that lawn machinery I've never seen in my life, and I do see a lot.*

DC: *I just bet you have. Where do you come from?*

JC: *I come from Thompson, Vermont. It's a small town outside Montpelier.*

DC: *That's interesting. I'm a born-and-bred Pennsylvanian. Moved here from New York. It's good to escape city life in my old age of retirement.*

JC: *I feel just the opposite. But then again, I'm still in my mid-twenties. I drive as fast as those cars that rush by. Sometimes I get caught, though.*

DC: *Well, you better just slow it down a bit there, young person. I don't want to see you in a body cast and me slapped with a lawsuit because you crashed into my tree.*

JC: *It's not like you've never been stopped by a cop.*

DC: *How would you know that? For all you know, I could've been the chief of police here.*

JC: *You sure don't look like a cop. What do you do for a living anyway?*

DC: *I was fighting in the war to make life good for people like you. Now I regret that if they're all like you. You know, I don't have to sit here and take this from you. I'm going inside.*

On Names and Naming

After reading portions of Jhumpa Lahiri's novel *The Namesake*, we talked about our own names, how we got them, what they mean, and whether or not we think they "fit" our personalities. Then we each took fictional names, checked the meaning of those names in a naming dictionary, and imagined a confrontation that might occur when each of our fictional characters discovered (or sought to discover) just how and why they got the names they did.

I slammed my bedroom door as loud as I could, hoping that my parents were still in the living room. My parents, of course, hadn't made an effort to apologize or comfort me. The conversation with them downstairs a couple of minutes ago, had gone like this:

 "Mom, I—"

 "Honey, shhh!"

 ". . . and now for only $9.99 each!" boomed the TV as a female model swished her unrealistically shiny hair.

 "Good, good," muttered my mother, her white, bony hands curled around the pen she was holding.

By Caeli

In the bitter, December wind Blythe could hardly keep her azure blue parka around her petite frame. She huddled beneath the warm sanctity the jacket provided, her mind on other things. She tried to pretend that she was still happy . . . Blythe was always supposed to be optimistic. She tried to push away the other thoughts of sadness and she focused on being cheerful to the point of delirium.

 She was standing on a street corner, trying to get a cab to take her to her dad's apartment. But she couldn't figure out why he wanted to see her now, it had always seemed that he was very busy. Abruptly a large, yellow taxi pulled up next to her. The friction of its wheels against the pavement sprayed her in numbingly cold rain water which fell from her face like tears. Instead of focusing on the cold, she thought about the sunny days when she and her father would play catch in the yard. She would never be able to catch his throws, so when he thought she wasn't looking, he would take a step forward so she could catch it.

"Where to, miss?" The cabdriver's inquiry brought her back from her memories.

"Oh . . . 168 Errol Avenue," Blythe replied hastily. The cabbie nodded with recognition and immediately started his engine. The car gave a smooth start as it began down the slippery road. Blythe gazed out the tinted window at the broken homes and unfurnished lawns as the cab bounced along the cracked streets. She was so deep in thought that it surprised her how quickly they arrived at her father's office.

It was an incredibly run-down building. The windows were covered with layers upon layers of dust. Someone had written "WASH ME" with their fingers on the dirty glass. Blythe quickly got out of the car and paid the driver. As she approached the rickety building she couldn't suppress the worry she felt for her father. It looked as though business wasn't going too well.

She approached the door in a state of false confidence, her hands jammed into her coat pockets. She noticed that the 6 on the address had fallen, leaving a faded silhouette against the peeling, crimson paint. She rang the doorbell.

After moments of silent waiting she simply walked in to find her father, or at least a wizened parody, staring at a TV set which showed a fuzzy, black-and-white picture. An absentminded expression adorned his weathered face.

"Daddy," she whispered softly. He looked up at her with a sad smile, almost a grimace. There was shame, hidden but still prominent, in the curve of his lips and the corner of his eyes.

"You wanted to see me?" Blythe stared hard at her father. Was that a look of grief etched on his face?

"Yes, Blythe, come sit down," he said almost warily. "Have you ever wondered where you got your name from?"

There was an explosion on the television screen. How ominous, Blythe thought wryly. After what seemed like hours she managed to meet her father's eyes, unable to understand the fear that this topic instilled in her.

"No, I haven't. What does my name mean?" she asked, feeling strangely defiant. Her father sighed, seemingly exhaling his pent-up sorrow in the process.

"As you know, Blythe means happy. Your mother wanted to name you this before she had to go to the institution." Blythe's mother had been forced to go to a mental institution shortly after her first and only daughter had been born.

"She wanted you to always be cheerful, no matter what befell you," he continued.

Blythe looked up quickly at her father, just in time to see a single tear rolling down his cheek. The subject of Blythe's mother had always been a hard one, and thus rarely discussed.

By Tiernan, Gabrielle, and Sarah

Kirsten slammed the sliding door of her parents' disgruntled beach house and jogged out into the early evening mist. When she got to the beach she looked around and lit a cigarette. She was supposed to meet her friend Miriam in three minutes. Kirsten walked up to the water and stared through the ever-moving waves at the minute crabs practicing ballet. As her eyes unfocused and she gazed vainly at her reflection—a blonde girl in baggy black clothes—another reflection approached behind her.

"Boo!" said Miriam.

"You've just turned seven. Grow up!" replied Kirsten.

Miriam growled, but was drowned out by the nearby church bells.

"*You know, your name means 'church,'*" *Miriam shot* back.

Kirsten groaned, grabbed Miriam's bike, [which was] *lying in the sand, and took off.*

By Madeline

As I walk home from school, the water slaps the sides of my *old, torn, and battered sneakers. Around the blue fabric* *water is running, sprinting, but it only seems to end up in* *the water mains, like planned. A sudden thought strikes me* *as I walk, stopping me in my tracks.* Was I planned like that? *I wonder. As I reflect on my miserable life, which it seems is* *only sinking more and more into the ocean of depression, I* *think,* Of course not. *After hearing my cheap sneakers slap* *the sidewalks of fourteen streets, my route home, I finally* *reach the house I live in, whose roof tiles are coming undone* *like a baby tooth hanging from a thread. Other fragments* *are missing from the house, such as the two small and square* *windows that are broken or have cracks like strands of silk.* *Also missing is the door, which has small holes in it where* *bullets had, while we were living here, been shot through.* *The windows have been covered in iron bars, but the door* *was never repaired for money's sake. I look in my denim* *sack, which is my book bag for school, for my key. It isn't in* *view as my eyes thoroughly search again and again. My fos-* *ter mother, Mary, will not be home for another five hours,* *and that means* 10:00. *That means I will sit out on my stoop* *until* 10:00 *tonight. It is* 5:00 *now. I wait.*

"*Going somewhere, Paloma?*" *I hear a voice say, which* *seems to make its way to my inner ear.*

The woman next door is sitting out on her stoop. Her *long white hair is loose and clings to her white nightgown.* *The woman, as I can see, has been sleeping. Still she looks* as though she has just finished watching a phenomenon, and is coming to a conclusion about what she has seen. Her gray eyes show her age, though her skin is free of wrinkles. She once told me it was from the vegetables her imam, or mother, made her eat at a young age. The woman's name is Georathia. I don't know much about her or where she comes from, only that she lives next door and can be good to talk to. I never have known how she knows my name, which is Paloma. "I got locked out," I tell her. She gives a nod that seems quite subtle, her eyes remaining open. Her gaze is on me, but it doesn't seem hard.

"That can be hard, can't it, if Mary won't be home for a few hours." Silence starts to echo. She keeps looking at me, but a change happens when she closes her eyes. I can see her lips forming a word, and then a sentence.

"Paloma, your father was very much obliged to give you to Mary, over the other foster families. I remember the night he brought you here. The clouds seemed purple that night, and the wind picked up, but it was not harsh. You looked five maybe, quite a change from the fourteen-year-old you've become. I remember when your father was young also, and he talked of airplanes. He always wanted an airplane of his own, just to fly. Even when I could hold him in my arms, when he was fragile, he played with airplanes. At our home, we had many models and books about airplanes. I talked to him the other day and he was flying for American Airlines, had a flight to Japan the next day. I love him so. Because of his love of flying, he named you Paloma. Your name means dove. He always knew you would fly away to a place better than he could have taken you."

Truly what I have just heard will lift me up, for I, like a dove, have flown into a beautiful place.

By Greta

Critical Junctures

We listened to audio recordings of turning points in the lives of athletes, politicians, and war heroes and then talked about turning points in our own lives. Working in groups of two or three, we then interviewed one another about those critical junctures, collecting as many details as we thought we might need to craft a first-person essay based on the details our partners provided. Daniel told John a story about taking care of a dog that barked all night. John told Daniel about being hit by a car while reading a book. Here are the essays each wrote about the other.

> *I saw it. It was a delight until night. It barked from 12:00 P.M to 6:00 A.M. I was awake all night. In the morning, I went to that dog. It bit me! It constantly bit me. I hated that dog.*
>
> > *By John*

> *I had been having a normal day reading a book, arguing with my sometimes annoying brother Jake. My brother had beckoned from across the street. I started to cross, reading my book peacefully. Suddenly a car, like a dark avatar, flew out of the twisting nether of the street into my side. I was thrown aside like an old doll, jolted into a pickup truck and thrown down. The driver of the demonic engine said he would be back after he parked his vehicle. He returned and asked how I was. I was driven to the hospital and got a neck brace. I asked if I could keep it, but they said no.*
>
> > *By Daniel*

Jake took the story that Jeremy told him about working at a horse show and wrote the following:

*It was the event that changed me. I could do anything that
a fourteen-year-old could. It was my first career experience.
I was the candy man at the local horse show. I didn't work
at the stand, but instead got to move around with a candy
package. I could go in front of the rides so everyone would
notice me. It was chilly and it rained but it never dampened
my spirits. The lemon-cutting job kept me there even longer
to enjoy the horse show. But I wasn't worked like a dog. I
got a break. I flirted with the attractive female customers. It
was quite busy and that let me meet more people. Also, the
hospital felt happiness. I donated my pay to them. These
were my finest nine days, the days I was a man.*

By Jake

Musical Influences

We were thinking about the role that music plays in movies and
about how music always suggests a certain mood, movement, or
possibility. We listened to Gregorian chants, to the experimental
work of the Argentine singer Juana Molina, and to "Ways That
Are Dark," a song cycle based on one of the founders of the Great
Smoky Mountains National Park. We developed descriptions of
plot or story inspired by the patterns in the music that we heard.
Jeremy heard one Juana Molina song as being the backdrop to
"the quiet scene in an action movie," while Sophie heard the mak-
ings of a Western tale.

*The president has recently announced that the United
States will go to war with Iraq. Certain soldiers have been
asked to fight in the war. Lt. Martin Thompson is one of
those soldiers, and he has just arrived in Iraq. It is the night
before the war. He walks into a small bar wearing military
dress uniform. He sits down and loosens his clothing. He*

orders a beer from the suspicious bartender, and while he is
drinking, he is also thinking, Was it worth it to join the
Army? *That is the question that worries him throughout the
whole drink, and even the next. Finally, after he finishes the
second drink, he decides that it was. He might die, he thinks,
but if he does, he will die a hero.*

By Jeremy

*Racing across the desert are two cowboys, a father and son.
They come to the edge of a cliff; no one is in sight. All the
two know is that they have to go north.*

"Gee, Papa, I think we are lost."

*"Charlie, there is no need to worry. We will get home
sooner or later."*

"But what about Mom? She needs us."

*"We'll make it, Charlie, just in time. She will wait before
going . . ."*

*Charlie dismounts and goes to the edge of the cliff to
have a look.*

*"Watch it, Charlie. We don't need two deaths in the
family."*

"Don't worry, Dad. . . . AAAaaawwwww."

"Charlie, Charlie, can you hear me? Are you okay?"

"Yes, Dad, but I think I broke my wrist."

"Can you climb out?"

"No, it's too high."

"Okay, wait there while I get the rope off Flim Flam."

By Sophie

Jake focused on the Gregorian chants and wrote the following:

*The monks in white habits are in two columns chanting.
The abbot is in the front of the church at the pulpit with the*

Holy Bible open. Finally, all enter and the praying ends. They then bow their heads in complete and total silence. The abbot then looks down at the Holy Bible. He opens his mouth. At first no sound comes out but then it arrives. "Let's thank the Lord for this beautiful day," he says, in a voice loud and full of feeling. He then says a prayer and dismisses the monks to their quiet, holy activities.

By Jake